THE MEAL PLAN MY DOCTOR SHOULD HAVE GIVEN ME

How I Took Control Of My Health One Bite At A Time

Riley N. Parker

CONTENTS

BREAKFAST:

LUNCH AND LIGHT MEALS:

DINNER & MAIN COURSE:

INTRODUCTION

Let me tell you about the day I realized my body was screaming for help

It was 2:30 PM on a Tuesday, and I was sitting in my car in the parking lot of my doctor's office, staring at a prescription bottle that was supposed to solve all my problems. Third medication this year. The inflammation markers in my blood work were off the charts—again. My joints ached like I'd aged twenty years overnight. My energy was non-existent by lunch every day. And my doctor, bless his heart, kept treating the symptoms while the fire inside my body kept raging.

That's when it hit me: I was managing a chronic illness, not healing from it.

Sound familiar? Maybe you're holding your own prescription bottle right now, wondering if there's more to this story. Maybe you've been told your symptoms are "just part of getting older" or "probably stress-related." Maybe you're like I was—frustrated, tired, and feeling like your own body has turned against you.

Here's what nobody tells you: you're not alone in this fight. According to recent research, chronic inflammation affects an estimated 60% of Americans. That's 3 out of every 5 people walking around with their bodies in a constant state of internal conflict. The Centers for Disease Control reports that chronic inflammatory diseases are responsible for 7 out of 10 deaths in the United States. We're talking about conditions like heart disease, cancer, chronic kidney disease, and stroke—diseases that often have inflammation as their common thread.

What inflammation really is—and why nobody talks about the chronic kind

Let's get something straight from the start: inflammation isn't always the villain. When you cut your finger or twist your ankle, that redness, heat, and swelling? That's acute inflammation, and it's actually your body's superhero response. It's calling in the cavalry to fight infection and heal tissue. This type of inflammation shows up fast, does its job, and then packs up and goes home. It's supposed to be temporary.

But chronic inflammation? That's a completely different beast, and it's the one we need to talk about.

Chronic inflammation happens when your immune system gets stuck in "attack mode." Instead of responding to a real threat and then calming down, it keeps sending out inflammatory signals day after day, month after month, sometimes for years. It's like having a car alarm that won't turn off—eventually, everyone stops paying attention to it, but the damage keeps happening in the background.

Here's the scary part: chronic inflammation is often silent. You might not even know it's happening until it's been wreaking havoc on your system for years. While acute inflammation announces itself with obvious symptoms, chronic inflammation whispers. It shows up as that persistent fatigue you can't shake, the brain fog that makes you feel like you're thinking through molasses, the joint stiffness that greets you every morning, or the digestive issues that have become your new normal.

The research is staggering. A study published in Nature Medicine found that chronic inflammation accelerates aging at the cellular level. Another study in the New England Journal of Medicine showed that people with elevated inflammatory markers had a 31% higher risk of heart attack, even when their cholesterol levels were normal. The Harvard School of Public Health has linked chronic inflammation to depression, with inflammatory cytokines literally changing brain chemistry.

But here's what really gets me fired up: most of this chronic inflammation is preventable. And often, it's reversible.

The moment I discovered food wasn't just fuel, it was medicine

I'll never forget the conversation that changed everything. I was sitting across from a functional medicine practitioner after months of feeling like garbage, and she said something that stopped me cold: "Your fork is either fighting disease or feeding it with every single bite."

Wait, what?

She explained that every time we eat, we're either adding kindling to the inflammatory fire in our bodies or helping to put it out. Food isn't just calories or macronutrients—it's information. It's sending signals to our genes, our immune system, and our inflammatory pathways.

This was revolutionary to me. I'd spent years thinking about food in terms of weight management or energy levels, but never as medicine. Turns out, the research backs this up in ways that would make your head spin.

A landmark study published in the Journal of the American College of Cardiology followed over 210,000 people for more than 32 years and found that those eating the most anti-inflammatory foods had a 13% lower risk of cardiovascular disease and an 18% lower risk of stroke. The Mediterranean diet—which is essentially an anti-inflammatory eating pattern—has been shown to reduce inflammatory markers by up to 20% in just eight weeks.

But it gets even more interesting. Research from Harvard Medical School shows that certain foods can increase inflammatory markers within hours of eating them. A single high-sugar, high-fat meal can spike inflammatory cytokines for up to four hours. On the flip side, foods rich in omega-3 fatty acids, antioxidants, and polyphenols can begin reducing inflammatory markers within days.

The National Institutes of Health has funded extensive research showing that dietary intervention can be as effective as medication for managing inflammatory conditions. In some cases, more effective. And unlike pharmaceuticals, the side effects of eating anti-inflammatory foods include better energy, clearer skin, improved mood, and enhanced cognitive function.

Why I'm sharing this journey with you (spoiler: because it changed everything)

Here's the thing—I'm not a naturally optimistic person. I'm the type who needs to see the research, understand the mechanism, and experience the results before I'm convinced of anything. So when I tell you that changing how I ate literally gave me my life back, I don't say it lightly.

Within six weeks of adopting an anti-inflammatory approach to eating, my energy levels stabilized. The afternoon crashes that had plagued me for years simply disappeared. My joint pain decreased by about 70%. My sleep improved. Even my mood felt more balanced. And my blood work? Those inflammatory markers that had been climbing for years finally started coming down.

But here's what really motivated me to write this book: I started talking to other people about what I'd learned, and I kept hearing the same stories over and over. People who'd been struggling with mysterious symptoms for years. Folks who'd been told their lab results were "normal" even though they felt awful. Individuals managing multiple chronic conditions who'd never been told that inflammation might be the common thread connecting them all.

The more I learned, the more frustrated I became with how little of this information reaches the people who need it most. The research exists. The solutions are available. But somehow, the connection between what we eat and how we feel gets lost in a healthcare system that's designed to treat symptoms rather than address root causes.

According to the American Heart Association, the average American consumes 17 teaspoons of added sugar per day—more than double the recommended amount. The typical Western diet has an omega-6 to omega-3 ratio of about 20:1, when research suggests it should be closer to 4:1 for optimal health. We're eating our way into chronic inflammation, and most of us don't even realize it.

But here's the hope in all of this: if we can eat our way into chronic inflammation, we can eat our way out of it too.

What we're going to figure out together in these pages

I'm not going to lie to you—this isn't a quick fix or a miracle cure. What I'm sharing with you is a comprehensive approach to understanding and addressing chronic inflammation through food and lifestyle changes. It's based on solid science, real-world application, and the experiences of thousands of people who've walked this path.

Together, we're going to explore why your body might be stuck in inflammatory mode and how to help it find its way back to balance. We'll dig into the specific foods that fan inflammatory flames and the ones that help extinguish them. You'll learn cooking methods that support healing and lifestyle practices that complement your dietary changes.

Most importantly, you'll discover that you have more control over your health than you might think. The power to influence your inflammatory status is literally at your fingertips—or more accurately, at the end of your fork.

We'll start with understanding the science behind inflammation and diet, because I believe you deserve to know not just what to do, but why it works. Then we'll get practical with meal planning, shopping lists, and recipes that actually taste good. Because let's be honest—if the food doesn't taste good, you're not going to stick with it, and sustainable change is what we're after here.

By the time you finish this book, you'll have the knowledge and tools to become your own health advocate. You'll understand how to read your body's signals, make informed choices about what you eat, and create an anti-inflammatory lifestyle that fits your real life, not some idealized version of it.

This journey changed everything for me, and I believe it can change everything for you too. Are you ready to find out what it feels like when your body stops fighting itself and starts working with you instead?

CHAPTER ONE: The Fire Inside—Why Your Body Might Be Fighting Itself

Here's what I wish someone had told me about inflammation years ago

Picture this: your immune system is like the world's most dedicated security team. When everything's working properly, they're vigilant but calm, ready to spring into action when there's a real threat. But what happens when your security team gets paranoid? When they start seeing enemies everywhere, even in the very building they're supposed to protect?

That's chronic inflammation in a nutshell.

I spent years thinking inflammation was just something that happened when you got injured or sick. Ice for swelling, rest for healing, and you're good to go. Nobody ever explained to me that inflammation could be happening inside my body 24/7, slowly damaging tissues and organs without me even knowing it.

Here's what I wish someone had sat me down and explained years ago: chronic inflammation is like having a small fire burning in your basement. You might not smell the smoke at first, but it's slowly damaging the foundation of your house. By the time you notice something's wrong, the fire has been burning for months or even years.

The medical term for this is "subclinical chronic inflammation"—basically, inflammation that's happening below the radar of obvious symptoms but above the level of normal. It's not dramatic enough to send you to the emergency room, but it's significant enough to slowly erode your health over time.

What really gets me is that we have blood tests that can measure inflammatory markers—things like C-reactive protein (CRP), interleukin-6, and tumor necrosis factor-alpha. But unless you're having a heart attack or dealing with an obvious inflammatory condition, most doctors don't routinely check these markers. It's like having a smoke detector in your basement but never changing the batteries.

The research that made me sit up and pay attention (and why it should matter to you)

Let me share the study that completely changed how I think about inflammation and health. It's called the CANTOS trial, published in the New England Journal of Medicine in 2017, and it's a game-changer.

Researchers followed over 10,000 people who had already survived a heart attack. Half received a powerful anti-inflammatory drug, and half received a placebo. Here's the kicker: both groups had normal cholesterol levels and were already on standard heart medications. The only difference was inflammation treatment.

The results? The group receiving anti-inflammatory treatment had a 15% reduction in cardiovascular events and a 17% reduction in stroke risk. This wasn't about cholesterol, blood pressure, or any of the usual suspects we blame for heart disease. This was purely about inflammation.

Dr. Paul Ridker, who led the study, called it "proof of concept that inflammation contributes to cardiovascular risk above and beyond cholesterol." Translation: inflammation isn't just a side effect of disease—it's often the driver.

But the research rabbit hole goes so much deeper. A massive meta-analysis published in the American Journal of Clinical Nutrition analyzed data from over 200 studies and found that people with the highest levels of inflammatory markers had:

- 42% higher risk of stroke
- 35% higher risk of heart disease
- 50% higher risk of diabetes
- 25% higher risk of certain cancers
- Significantly increased risk of depression and cognitive decline

The Nurses' Health Study, which followed over 80,000 women for more than 20 years, found that those with the highest inflammatory markers were 70% more likely to develop diabetes, even after accounting for weight, exercise, and family history.

Here's what really blew my mind: research from the University of California San Diego showed that chronic inflammation can actually change how your genes are expressed. It's called "inflammaging"—the idea that chronic inflammation accelerates cellular aging. People with higher inflammatory markers have shorter telomeres (the protective caps on chromosomes), which is essentially a measure of biological aging.

A groundbreaking study published in Nature found that reducing systemic inflammation could add years to your life. Not just years of living, but years of healthy living. We're talking about compression of morbidity—staying healthier longer and having a shorter period of illness before death.

But here's the research finding that really hit home for me: a study from Harvard School of Public Health found that dietary patterns alone could reduce inflammatory markers by 20-30% within just 8-12 weeks. No medications, no invasive procedures—just changing what people ate.

Real talk: How many of these sound familiar?

Okay, let's get personal for a minute. I'm going to list some symptoms, and I want you to honestly think about whether any of these ring a bell. Don't worry—this isn't a diagnostic tool, and I'm not trying to scare you. But these are the whispers chronic inflammation uses to get your attention before it starts shouting.

That afternoon energy crash that feels like hitting a wall

You know the one I'm talking about. It's 2 PM, you've had a decent breakfast and lunch, maybe even some coffee, but suddenly you feel like someone pulled your plug. It's not just tiredness—it's like your body just decided to quit on you. You find yourself reaching for sugar or caffeine just to make it through the rest of the day.

This isn't normal, despite what our culture tells us. Research shows that inflammatory cytokines directly interfere with cellular energy production. When your body is fighting chronic inflammation, it's diverting energy away from normal functions just to keep up with the inflammatory response. A study in the journal Brain, Behavior, and Immunity found that people with higher inflammatory markers experienced significantly more fatigue, even when other health factors were accounted for.

Waking up stiff like you're 90 when you're nowhere close

That morning stiffness that takes 20-30 minutes to work out of your joints? The feeling like your body aged 20 years overnight? That's not just "sleeping wrong" or "getting older."

Morning stiffness lasting more than 30 minutes is actually one of the clinical criteria doctors use to assess inflammatory arthritis. But you don't need a diagnosis of arthritis to experience inflammation in your joints and muscles. Research from the University of Pittsburgh found that people with elevated C-reactive protein levels were significantly more likely to report morning stiffness and joint discomfort, even without any diagnosed joint conditions.

Brain fog that makes you forget words mid-sentence

This one really gets to me because it's so frustrating and yet so common. You're in the middle of a conversation and suddenly the word you're looking for just... disappears. Or you walk into a room and can't remember why you went there. Or you read the same paragraph three times and still don't know what it said.

The research on neuroinflammation is absolutely fascinating and terrifying. Studies using brain imaging show that people with higher systemic inflammatory markers have increased inflammation in brain tissue. This neuroinflammation interferes with neurotransmitter production, disrupts sleep patterns, and affects memory consolidation.

A study published in Neurology followed over 12,000 people for 20 years and found that those with the highest inflammatory markers in midlife had significantly smaller brain volumes and worse cognitive function in later life. The inflammation was literally shrinking their brains.

Skin that just won't cooperate no matter what you try

Acne in your 30s, 40s, or beyond. Eczema that flares up for no apparent reason. Rosacea that makes you look perpetually sunburned. Psoriasis patches that seem to have a mind of their own. Or just dull, lifeless skin that makes you look tired even when you're not.

Your skin is your body's largest organ, and it's often the first place inflammation shows up visually. Research shows that people with inflammatory skin conditions have elevated systemic inflammatory markers, not just local skin inflammation. A study in the Journal of Investigative Dermatology found that reducing systemic inflammation through diet improved skin conditions in 73% of participants within 12 weeks.

But here's what's really interesting: even people without diagnosed skin conditions often see dramatic improvements in skin clarity, texture, and radiance when they address chronic inflammation. It's like your skin finally gets permission to do its job properly.

The conditions that finally make sense when you understand inflammation

Once you understand that chronic inflammation is like a slow-burning fire in your body, so many seemingly unrelated health issues suddenly start making sense. It's like finally finding the missing piece of a puzzle you've been working on for years.

Autoimmune Conditions: When Your Security System Goes Rogue

Conditions like rheumatoid arthritis, lupus, multiple sclerosis, inflammatory bowel disease, and psoriasis are all characterized by the immune system attacking healthy tissue. But here's what's wild: research shows that dietary intervention can often reduce symptoms and slow progression of these conditions. The American College of Rheumatology now acknowledges that anti-inflammatory diets can be as effective as some medications for managing rheumatoid arthritis symptoms.

Heart Disease: More Than Just Cholesterol

We've been so focused on cholesterol that we've missed the inflammation connection. But research now shows that people with high cholesterol and low inflammation have much lower heart disease risk than people with normal cholesterol and high inflammation. The American Heart Association has officially recognized inflammation as a major risk factor for cardiovascular disease.

Type 2 Diabetes: The Inflammatory Connection

Type 2 diabetes isn't just about blood sugar—it's fundamentally an inflammatory condition. Chronic inflammation interferes with insulin signaling, leading to insulin resistance. Research from the Joslin Diabetes Center shows that reducing inflammation can improve insulin sensitivity even before significant weight loss occurs.

Depression and Anxiety: The Mind-Body Connection

This one surprised me the most. Research shows that about 30% of people with depression have elevated inflammatory markers. Anti-inflammatory treatments have been shown to improve depression symptoms in some people, even when traditional antidepressants haven't worked.

Digestive Issues: The Gut-Inflammation Loop

IBS, IBD, GERD, and other digestive problems often involve inflammation in the digestive tract. But here's the kicker: gut inflammation can trigger systemic inflammation throughout the body, and systemic inflammation can worsen gut problems. It's a vicious cycle that dietary intervention can help break.

Cancer: The Long-Term Risk

Chronic inflammation creates an environment that promotes cancer development and progression. The American Cancer Society estimates that chronic inflammation contributes to about 25% of all cancers. While anti-inflammatory eating isn't a cancer cure, research shows it can significantly reduce cancer risk.

Why this isn't just another diet book (because honestly, who needs another one of those?)

I know, I know. You've probably read other health books that promised to solve all your problems if you just followed their specific plan. Maybe you've tried elimination diets, detoxes, or the latest trendy eating plan. Maybe some of them even worked for a while before you found yourself back where you started.

Here's why this is different: we're not chasing weight loss or trying to fit into a specific dietary ideology. We're addressing a biological process that underlies most chronic health issues. We're not just changing what you eat—we're changing how your body responds to what you eat.

The anti-inflammatory approach isn't a fad diet with arbitrary rules. It's based on decades of research into how specific foods and nutrients affect inflammatory pathways in your body. The goal isn't to restrict everything you enjoy—it's to understand which foods support your body's natural healing processes and which ones work against them.

This isn't about perfection or deprivation. It's about making informed choices based on how different foods make you feel, not just how they taste or how convenient they are. It's about understanding that every meal is an opportunity to either support your health or undermine it.

Most importantly, this approach is sustainable because it's based on adding healing foods to your life, not just removing problematic ones. You'll discover foods that are genuinely delicious and satisfying while also being powerfully anti-inflammatory. You'll learn to cook in ways that enhance the healing properties of your ingredients.

The research backs this up: people who follow anti-inflammatory eating patterns long-term don't just have better health markers—they report higher levels of energy, better mood, improved sleep, and an overall better quality of life. They're not suffering through a restrictive diet—they're thriving on a way of eating that makes them feel genuinely good.

And here's the best part: unlike restrictive diets that require willpower to maintain, anti-inflammatory eating becomes self-reinforcing. Once you experience how good you can feel when chronic inflammation calms down, going back to inflammatory foods feels like volunteering to feel awful. Your body becomes your best motivator.

So no, this isn't just another diet book. This is a roadmap to understanding your body's inflammatory responses and using that knowledge to reclaim your health, energy, and vitality. It's about becoming an active participant in your own healing rather than a passive recipient of whatever symptoms show up.

Ready to put out that fire that's been burning in your basement? Let's keep going.

CHAPTER TWO: Could This Be You? (The People I Meet Every Day)

The stories that break my heart—and give me hope

Every time I speak at a health conference or workshop, the same thing happens. During the break, people approach me with that look—you know the one. It's equal parts desperation and hope, like they're afraid to believe things could be different but can't help hoping anyway.

Last month, a woman named Louise came up to me after my presentation. She looked exhausted despite her carefully applied makeup and pressed business attire. "I've been to seven doctors in two years," she said quietly. "They keep telling me my labs are normal, but I feel like I'm dying inside. I can barely make it through a workday without wanting to cry from exhaustion."

Three weeks later, she emailed me: "I'm sleeping through the night for the first time in months. My afternoon crashes are gone. I actually have energy to play with my kids after work. I can't believe something as simple as changing what I eat could make this much difference."

Then there's Michael, a 45-year-old contractor who'd been dealing with joint pain so severe he was considering changing careers. "I thought I just had to live with it," he told me. "I'm in construction—aches and pains come with the territory, right?" Wrong. After eight weeks of anti-inflammatory eating, his pain levels dropped by 80%. He's back to working full days without needing ibuprofen to get through them.

These aren't miracle stories or one-off coincidences. I hear variations of them every single week because chronic inflammation is that common, and the solution is that accessible. The tragedy is how many people are suffering unnecessarily because they don't know inflammation could be the thread connecting all their seemingly unrelated symptoms.

The hope is that once you understand this connection, you have the power to do something about it.

If you're dealing with mystery symptoms that doctors can't quite pin down

This might be the most frustrating category of all. You know something's wrong. You feel awful, but your blood work comes back "normal." You're told it's stress, or hormones, or just part of getting older. You start to wonder if you're imagining things or being dramatic.

You're not imagining anything. And you're definitely not being dramatic.

The problem is that standard blood work doesn't typically include inflammatory markers unless you have an obvious inflammatory condition. Your complete blood count might be perfect, your cholesterol acceptable, your thyroid function normal—but nobody's checking your C-reactive protein, interleukin-6, or tumor necrosis factor levels.

It's like going to a mechanic because your car is making a weird noise, and they check the oil and tire pressure but never look under the hood where the actual problem is happening.

Research from the Mayo Clinic shows that up to 40% of people with symptoms suggestive of inflammatory conditions have normal routine lab work but elevated inflammatory markers when specifically tested. A study published in the Journal of Inflammation Research found that people with "medically unexplained symptoms" had significantly higher levels of inflammatory cytokines compared to healthy controls.

The mystery symptoms that often point to chronic inflammation:

- Persistent fatigue that doesn't improve with rest
- Brain fog or difficulty concentrating
- Joint pain or stiffness without obvious cause
- Digestive issues that come and go
- Skin problems that don't respond to typical treatments
- Sleep disturbances or non-restorative sleep
- Mood changes, anxiety, or mild depression
- Frequent infections or slow healing
- Unexplained headaches
- Muscle aches and pains

The Cleveland Clinic recently published data showing that 73% of patients with these types of symptoms had measurable improvement within 6-8 weeks of adopting an anti-inflammatory diet, even when conventional treatments had failed.

Here's what I want you to understand: just because your doctor can't find an obvious cause for your symptoms doesn't mean the cause doesn't exist. It might just mean you're looking in the wrong place. Chronic inflammation is often the hidden culprit behind mystery symptoms that seem to have no medical explanation.

When your family tree reads like a medical textbook

Does this sound familiar? Heart disease runs in your family. So does diabetes. And arthritis. Maybe there's some cancer history, a few autoimmune conditions, and more than one person dealing with depression or anxiety. You look at your family medical history and think, "Well, I'm screwed genetically."

Here's the truth that nobody talks about: genetics loads the gun, but lifestyle pulls the trigger.

The Meal Plan My Doctor Should Have Given me

The field of epigenetics has revolutionized our understanding of how genes work. Your genes don't determine your destiny—they determine your tendencies. Whether those tendencies become reality depends largely on how you live, what you eat, and how you manage stress.

Research from Harvard Medical School found that people with strong genetic predispositions to inflammatory diseases could reduce their risk by up to 50% through anti-inflammatory lifestyle choices. The Nurses' Health Study, which followed over 120,000 people for more than 30 years, showed that dietary patterns had a stronger influence on disease development than family history in many cases.

The inflammatory genetic patterns I see most often:

- Multiple family members with autoimmune conditions
- Heart disease affecting multiple generations
- Type 2 diabetes running through the family line
- Cancer clusters, especially hormone-related cancers
- Mental health issues across family members
- Digestive problems being "normal" in your family
- Joint problems that everyone just accepts as inevitable

But here's the hopeful part: a study published in Nature Genetics found that anti-inflammatory diets could actually change gene expression within 12 weeks. People with genetic predispositions to inflammatory diseases saw their inflammatory genes "turn down" and their protective genes "turn up" through dietary intervention alone.

I think about Maria, whose family history included rheumatoid arthritis (grandmother), lupus (aunt), Crohn's disease (sister), and heart disease (father). She came to me convinced she was destined for autoimmune disease because she was already experiencing joint pain and digestive issues in her early thirties.

Two years later, her inflammatory markers are in the optimal range, her joint pain is gone, and her digestive issues have resolved. She's broken the family pattern not through medication or drastic measures, but by giving her genes a different environment to express themselves in.

Your family history isn't your destiny—it's your wake-up call to be proactive about inflammation before it becomes a bigger problem.

For my fellow warriors battling autoimmune conditions

If you're dealing with an autoimmune condition, you're already intimately familiar with inflammation. You probably know your inflammatory markers, understand flare-ups, and have experienced the frustrating cycle of medications that help for a while and then seem to lose effectiveness.

First, let me be crystal clear: I'm not suggesting you abandon medical treatment or stop working with your rheumatologist, gastroenterologist, or other specialists. What I'm suggesting is that you add another powerful tool to your toolkit.

The research on diet and autoimmune conditions is compelling. A systematic review published in Nutrients journal analyzed 23 studies on dietary interventions for autoimmune conditions and found significant improvements in disease activity, quality of life, and inflammatory markers across multiple conditions.

The autoimmune-inflammation connection:

Rheumatoid arthritis patients following anti-inflammatory diets showed 25-40% reductions in joint pain and swelling, according to research from the Arthritis Foundation. Some participants were able to reduce their medication dosages under medical supervision.

People with inflammatory bowel disease saw 60% reductions in flare-ups and significantly improved quality of life scores when following structured anti-inflammatory eating plans, based on research from the Crohn's & Colitis Foundation.

Psoriasis patients experienced average 45% improvements in skin clearing within 12 weeks of dietary intervention, according to studies published in the Journal of the American Academy of Dermatology.

Multiple sclerosis patients showed slower disease progression and fewer relapses when following anti-inflammatory diets rich in omega-3 fatty acids and antioxidants, based on research from the National MS Society.

But beyond the statistics, what really motivates me are stories like Jennifer's. She'd been dealing with rheumatoid arthritis for eight years, trying various medications with limited success and significant side effects. Within four months of adopting an anti-inflammatory approach, her morning stiffness decreased from two hours to fifteen minutes. Her energy levels improved dramatically. Her rheumatologist was amazed by her inflammatory marker improvements and was able to reduce one of her medications.

Or David, who'd been battling Crohn's disease for over a decade. He'd had multiple surgeries and was facing another one when he decided to try dietary intervention as a last resort. Eighteen months later, his colonoscopy showed significant healing of his intestinal lining, and he's been in remission ever since.

These aren't "miraculous cures"—they're examples of what can happen when you address the underlying inflammatory processes that drive autoimmune conditions.

Athletes who want to recover like they did in their twenties

This category is close to my heart because it's where I first discovered the power of anti-inflammatory eating. I was a weekend warrior dealing with longer recovery times, more frequent injuries, and that general feeling that my body just wasn't bouncing back like it used to.

Athletic performance and recovery are fundamentally about managing inflammation. Exercise creates controlled inflammatory stress that, when properly managed, leads to adaptation and improved performance. But when you add chronic dietary inflammation to exercise-induced inflammation, you get a recipe for poor recovery, frequent injuries, and declining performance.

Research from the International Society of Sports Nutrition shows that athletes following anti-inflammatory diets have:

- 32% faster recovery times between training sessions
- 28% fewer overuse injuries
- 15% improvements in endurance performance
- Better sleep quality and mood stability
- Reduced markers of exercise-induced oxidative stress

The athlete inflammation trap:

Many athletes unknowingly sabotage their recovery through inflammatory food choices. That post-workout protein shake with artificial ingredients, the quick fast-food meal between training sessions, the reliance on energy drinks and bars loaded with inflammatory oils and sweeteners—these choices create systemic inflammation that interferes with the body's natural recovery processes.

Professional sports teams are catching on. The Los Angeles Lakers, New England Patriots, and several Olympic training centers now employ nutritionists who specifically focus on anti-inflammatory eating strategies. The results speak for themselves: fewer injuries, faster recovery, and career longevity.

Take Mark, a 42-year-old triathlete who was considering giving up competitive racing because his recovery times had doubled and he was dealing with chronic knee pain. Within six weeks of cleaning up his diet and eliminating inflammatory foods, his recovery improved dramatically. Six months later, he posted a personal best at an Ironman event—at age 43.

Or Lisa, a recreational runner who couldn't understand why she was getting injured so frequently in her late thirties. Turns out, her post-run recovery routine included inflammatory foods that were preventing proper tissue repair. Once she switched to anti-inflammatory recovery nutrition, her injury rate dropped by 75%.

The beauty of anti-inflammatory eating for athletes is that it's not about restriction—it's about optimization. You're not eating less; you're eating smarter. Foods that taste great and provide sustainable energy while supporting recovery and reducing injury risk.

Anyone who's tired of feeling tired all the time

Chronic fatigue might be the most common symptom I encounter, and it's also one of the most dismissed by traditional medicine. If your thyroid is normal and you're not anemic, you're often told your fatigue is just stress, depression, or part of getting older.

But research shows that chronic inflammation is one of the primary drivers of persistent fatigue. Inflammatory cytokines directly interfere with cellular energy production, disrupt sleep patterns, and affect neurotransmitter function—all of which contribute to that bone-deep exhaustion that rest doesn't seem to fix.

A groundbreaking study published in Brain, Behavior, and Immunity followed over 3,000 people for five years and found that those with elevated inflammatory markers were 40% more likely to develop chronic fatigue, regardless of age, weight, or other health factors.

The inflammation-fatigue connection:

When your body is fighting chronic inflammation, it's like having multiple apps running in the background on your phone—your battery drains faster even when you're not actively using it. Your immune system is constantly working, your liver is processing inflammatory byproducts, and your cells are dealing with oxidative stress. All of this requires energy that would otherwise be available for normal daily activities.

The mitochondria—your cellular power plants—are particularly vulnerable to inflammatory damage. Research from Johns Hopkins shows that chronic inflammation can reduce mitochondrial efficiency by up to 40%, directly impacting your energy production at the cellular level.

But here's the hopeful part: energy improvements are often one of the first things people notice when they adopt anti-inflammatory eating. Unlike the fatigue that comes from calorie restriction or extreme dieting, anti-inflammatory eating actually supports cellular energy production.

I think about Emma, a working mom who described her fatigue as "feeling like I'm moving through molasses all day." She'd tried everything—more sleep, exercise, stress management, even therapy for what her doctor thought might be depression. Nothing helped until she addressed the inflammatory foods in her diet. Within three weeks, she had sustained energy throughout the day for the first time in years.

Or Robert, a 55-year-old executive who was convinced his crushing fatigue was just the price of a demanding career. It turned out that his daily inflammatory habits—fast food lunches, multiple energy drinks, late-night processed snacks—were creating systemic inflammation that was literally draining his energy. Six weeks after changing his eating patterns, he felt like he'd gotten his life back.

The energy that comes from reducing chronic inflammation isn't the jittery, artificial boost you get from caffeine or sugar. It's steady, sustainable energy that carries you through the day without crashes or the need for constant stimulation.

The skeptics (I was one too—here's what changed my mind)

I get it. Really, I do. When someone tells you that changing what you eat can dramatically improve your health, your first instinct is probably skepticism. Especially if you've tried other dietary approaches before without lasting success.

I was the biggest skeptic of all. I'm the type of person who needs to see peer-reviewed research, understand the mechanisms, and experience the results personally before I'm convinced of anything. When a colleague first suggested that my chronic symptoms might be related to inflammation and diet, my internal response was basically, "Here we go with another food fad."

What changed my mind wasn't testimonials or before-and-after photos—it was data.

The research on inflammation and diet is extensive, rigorous, and published in top-tier medical journals. We're not talking about cherry-picked studies or preliminary findings. We're talking about large-scale, long-term research from institutions like Harvard, Mayo Clinic, and Johns Hopkins.

The Meal Plan My Doctor Should Have Given me

The Mediterranean Diet Study, published in the New England Journal of Medicine, followed over 7,400 people for nearly five years and found that anti-inflammatory eating reduced cardiovascular events by 30%—so dramatically that they stopped the study early because it would have been unethical to continue giving some participants the less effective diet.

The PREDIMED study showed that anti-inflammatory eating patterns reduced diabetes risk by 52% in high-risk individuals. The Nurses' Health Study demonstrated 42% reductions in stroke risk. These aren't small, marginal improvements—these are the kinds of results that pharmaceutical companies spend billions trying to achieve.

But here's what really convinced me: the mechanism makes perfect biological sense.

We know that certain foods trigger inflammatory pathways in the body. We know that chronic inflammation contributes to most major diseases. We know that other foods contain compounds that actively reduce inflammation. It's not mysterious or magical—it's basic biochemistry.

The skeptical part of me also appreciated that anti-inflammatory eating isn't about restriction or deprivation. It's not about eliminating entire food groups or following arbitrary rules. It's about understanding how different foods affect your body's inflammatory responses and making choices based on that knowledge.

What finally sealed the deal for me was my own experience.

Within six weeks of adopting anti-inflammatory eating principles, my energy levels stabilized, my joint pain decreased significantly, my sleep improved, and my mood felt more balanced. My inflammatory markers, which had been elevated for years, finally came into the normal range.

But more importantly, I felt like myself again for the first time in years. Not a hyped-up, artificially energized version of myself, but genuinely healthy and vital.

The other thing that convinced this skeptic? The approach is completely reversible and risk-free. Unlike medications that can have serious side effects, or extreme diets that can cause nutritional deficiencies, anti-inflammatory eating is simply choosing foods that support your body's natural healing processes. The worst thing that can happen is you eat more vegetables and fewer processed foods.

If you're skeptical, I respect that. In fact, I encourage it. Don't take my word for anything—try it for yourself and pay attention to how you feel. Track your energy levels, sleep quality, joint comfort, and overall sense of well-being. Let your own experience be the judge.

The beautiful thing about addressing chronic inflammation through diet is that you don't have to believe it will work for it to work. Your body's inflammatory pathways will respond to anti-inflammatory foods whether you're convinced or not.

So here's my challenge to the skeptics: Give it eight weeks. Not half-heartedly, but genuinely committed to the process. Track how you feel, not just how you look. Pay attention to energy levels, sleep quality, mood, and any chronic symptoms you've been dealing with.

If you don't notice significant improvements, you can go back to eating however you want with the knowledge that you gave it a fair shot. But I'm willing to bet that you'll be surprised by how much better you can feel when you stop feeding the inflammatory fire and start supporting your body's natural healing processes.

Your skepticism might just turn into your strongest motivation, like it did for me.

CHAPTER THREE: The Foods That Betrayed Us (and Why We Never Saw it Coming)

The grocery store aisles that became my enemy (and probably yours too)

I used to think I was a pretty smart shopper. I read labels, avoided obviously unhealthy foods, and filled my cart with items that seemed reasonable. Whole grain bread, lean protein, low-fat dairy, heart-healthy oils. I even bought organic when I could afford it, feeling virtuous about my choices.

Looking back, I realize I was playing a game where nobody had explained the rules to me.

The middle aisles of the grocery store—you know, the ones packed with boxes, bags, and bottles—had become a minefield of inflammatory ingredients disguised as convenient, affordable food options. The worst part? Many of these foods were marketed as healthy choices.

That "heart-healthy" margarine? Loaded with inflammatory omega-6 oils and often trans fats. The whole grain bread I was so proud of buying? Packed with high-fructose corn syrup, inflammatory preservatives, and enough sodium to make your blood pressure monitor weep. The protein bars I grabbed for quick energy? More like inflammation bars wrapped in clever marketing.

According to the American Heart Association, the average American gets 60% of their calories from ultra-processed foods—foods that have been so altered from their original state that they barely resemble anything that grew from the ground or walked the earth. A landmark study published in the BMJ followed over 100,000 people for five years and found that every 10% increase in ultra-processed food consumption was associated with a 12% higher risk of cancer and a 13% higher risk of cardiovascular disease.

But here's what really gets me: we didn't choose this. The food industry spent decades and billions of dollars figuring out how to make processed foods irresistible, shelf-stable, and addictive. They hired neuroscientists to create "bliss points"—the perfect combination of sugar, salt, and fat that triggers dopamine release and keeps you coming back for more.

Meanwhile, they hired marketing experts to convince us these foods were not just acceptable, but beneficial. "Part of a complete breakfast." "Heart-healthy." "Natural flavors." "Fortified with vitamins." We were systematically taught to trust processed food manufacturers with our health, and most of us never questioned it.

The result? Chronic inflammation rates have skyrocketed alongside processed food consumption. Research from Harvard School of Public Health shows a direct correlation between ultra-processed food intake and inflammatory marker levels. People in the highest quartile of processed food consumption had 47% higher levels of C-reactive protein compared to those eating mostly whole foods.

Let's talk about sugar—the sweet saboteur hiding everywhere

Sugar is probably the most insidious inflammatory ingredient in our food supply, partly because it's everywhere and partly because we've been conditioned to think of it as harmless. "It's just empty calories," we tell ourselves. "I'll just work it off later."

But sugar isn't just empty calories—it's actively inflammatory. When you consume sugar, especially in large amounts or without fiber to slow absorption, it triggers a cascade of inflammatory responses throughout your body.

Here's what happens: sugar spikes your blood glucose, which triggers insulin release. High glucose levels also promote the formation of advanced glycation end products (AGEs)—compounds that directly trigger inflammatory pathways. Meanwhile, fructose (which makes up half of table sugar and most of high-fructose corn syrup) is processed almost exclusively by your liver, where it can trigger inflammatory cytokine production and contribute to fatty liver disease.

Research published in the American Journal of Clinical Nutrition found that people consuming high amounts of added sugar had inflammatory marker levels 87% higher than those with low sugar intake. Another study in the Journal of Nutrition showed that a single high-sugar meal could spike inflammatory markers for up to four hours.

But here's the real kicker: the average American consumes 17 teaspoons of added sugar per day. The American Heart Association recommends no more than 6 teaspoons for women and 9 for men. We're consuming nearly double the recommended amount, and most of us don't even realize it because sugar is hiding everywhere.

The sugar hiding places that shocked me:

- A single tablespoon of ketchup contains 1 teaspoon of sugar
- Flavored yogurt can contain up to 6 teaspoons of sugar per serving
- A seemingly healthy granola bar often contains 3-4 teaspoons
- Pasta sauce typically contains 2-3 teaspoons per half-cup serving
- Salad dressings can contain 1-2 teaspoons per tablespoon
- Even "savory" foods like crackers, bread, and canned soup are loaded with added sugars

The food industry uses over 60 different names for sugar on ingredient labels. High-fructose corn syrup, dextrose, maltose, rice syrup, agave nectar, cane juice, fruit juice concentrate—they're all sugar, and they're all inflammatory.

What really opened my eyes was a study from the University of California San Francisco showing that sugar consumption directly correlates with cellular aging. People with higher sugar intake had shorter telomeres—the protective caps on chromosomes that indicate biological age. Sugar wasn't just making people sick; it was literally aging them faster.

But here's what gives me hope: research shows that reducing sugar intake can decrease inflammatory markers within just two weeks. Your taste buds adapt quickly too. Foods that seemed normally sweet start tasting cloyingly sweet once you reduce your sugar intake. Your body literally recalibrates its expectations.

Those "healthy" oils that aren't so healthy after all

This one really got to me because I thought I was making smart choices. I'd switched from butter to vegetable oil for cooking, used margarine instead of butter, and specifically bought products labeled "made with heart-healthy oils." I was following conventional wisdom and doing what I thought was best for my health.

Turns out, I was pouring liquid inflammation into my body.

The problem with most vegetable oils—corn oil, soybean oil, safflower oil, sunflower oil, and canola oil—is that they're extremely high in omega-6 fatty acids. Now, omega-6 fats aren't inherently bad; we need some of them. The problem is the ratio.

Our ancestors consumed omega-6 and omega-3 fatty acids in roughly equal proportions. Today, the average American consumes them in a ratio of about 20:1 or even 30:1. This massive imbalance promotes inflammation throughout the body because omega-6 fats are the building blocks of pro-inflammatory compounds, while omega-3 fats are the building blocks of anti-inflammatory compounds.

Research published in Biomedicine & Pharmacotherapy found that people with omega-6 to omega-3 ratios higher than 4:1 had significantly elevated inflammatory markers and higher rates of cardiovascular disease, arthritis, and autoimmune conditions.

But it gets worse. Most vegetable oils are heavily processed using high heat, chemical solvents, and bleaching agents. This processing creates trans fats (even in oils labeled "trans fat free") and oxidizes the oils, making them even more inflammatory. A study in the Journal of Nutritional Biochemistry showed that heated vegetable oils produce over 100 different toxic compounds, many of which directly trigger inflammatory pathways.

The oils I learned to avoid:

- Soybean oil (found in most processed foods)
- Corn oil (often labeled as "vegetable oil")
- Canola oil (despite marketing as heart-healthy)
- Safflower and sunflower oils (unless specifically labeled high-oleic)
- Cottonseed oil (heavily processed and often GMO)
- Any oil that's been hydrogenated or partially hydrogenated

The food industry loves these oils because they're cheap, shelf-stable, and virtually flavorless. They're in almost every processed food, restaurant meal, and packaged snack. According to the USDA, soybean oil alone accounts for about 7% of calories in the average American diet.

What really convinced me to change was research from the NIH showing that simply switching from high omega-6 oils to more balanced fats could reduce inflammatory markers by 25-40% within eight weeks, without changing anything else about the diet.

Why the milk that did your body good might not be doing you good

This was a hard one for me to accept. I grew up with "Got Milk?" campaigns and genuinely believed dairy was essential for strong bones and good health. I drank milk with meals, ate yogurt for probiotics, and used cheese liberally in cooking.

But here's what I learned: the dairy we consume today isn't the same as the dairy our grandparents consumed. Modern dairy production has created a product that's inflammatory for many people, even those who aren't technically lactose intolerant.

The inflammatory issues with modern dairy:

Most commercial dairy comes from cows fed inflammatory diets high in corn and soy, kept in confinement, and given hormones and antibiotics. This creates milk with higher levels of inflammatory omega-6 fats and lower levels of anti-inflammatory omega-3s compared to grass-fed dairy.

The homogenization process—which makes milk look uniformly white and prevents cream separation—breaks fat molecules into smaller particles that may be more likely to trigger immune responses. Research published in the European Journal of Clinical Nutrition found that people consuming homogenized dairy had higher levels of inflammatory markers compared to those consuming non-homogenized dairy.

A1 beta-casein, a protein found in most commercial dairy, breaks down into a compound called BCM-7 during digestion. Studies suggest BCM-7 may trigger inflammatory responses and contribute to digestive issues, even in people who don't have obvious lactose intolerance.

The research that opened my eyes:

A study published in the Journal of Nutrition found that people consuming more than two servings of dairy per day had 35% higher levels of inflammatory markers compared to those consuming less than one serving per day.

Research from Harvard School of Public Health showed that countries with the highest dairy consumption actually had higher rates of osteoporosis, contradicting the "strong bones" narrative we've been sold.

A comprehensive review in Critical Reviews in Food Science and Nutrition found that dairy consumption was associated with increased inflammation in 52% of studies reviewed, while only 15% found anti-inflammatory effects.

The Meal Plan My Doctor Should Have Given me

But here's the interesting part: not all dairy is created equal. Studies show that dairy from grass-fed, pasture-raised animals has a completely different inflammatory profile. Grass-fed dairy contains higher levels of anti-inflammatory omega-3 fats, conjugated linoleic acid (CLA), and beneficial nutrients.

Research published in Food Chemistry found that grass-fed dairy had 62% more omega-3 fatty acids and 18% higher levels of CLA compared to conventional dairy. People consuming grass-fed dairy showed lower inflammatory markers compared to those consuming conventional dairy.

The processed meat problem nobody wants to acknowledge

I love a good burger as much as the next person, but I had to face the facts about processed meats. We're talking about deli meats, hot dogs, bacon, sausages, and any meat that's been preserved, cured, or heavily processed.

The World Health Organization classified processed meats as a Group 1 carcinogen—the same category as tobacco and asbestos. That got my attention. The American Institute for Cancer Research estimates that avoiding processed meats could prevent about 68,000 cases of colorectal cancer annually in the United States alone.

But the cancer risk is just part of the story. Processed meats are inflammatory for several reasons:

They're loaded with sodium nitrates and nitrites, preservatives that form nitrosamines in the body—compounds that directly trigger inflammatory pathways and DNA damage.

They contain advanced glycation end products (AGEs) formed during high-heat processing. AGEs bind to receptors in your body and trigger inflammatory cascades.

Most processed meats are made from conventionally raised animals fed inflammatory diets, resulting in meat with poor omega fatty acid profiles.

They often contain inflammatory oils, artificial flavors, and other additives that contribute to systemic inflammation.

Research published in the American Journal of Clinical Nutrition found that people consuming the most processed meat had inflammatory marker levels 28% higher than those consuming the least. Another study in Circulation showed that each daily serving of processed meat increased the risk of heart disease by 42% and diabetes by 19%.

The processed meats causing the most inflammation:

- Deli meats (turkey, ham, roast beef, etc.)
- Hot dogs and sausages
- Bacon (conventional, not nitrate-free)
- Pepperoni and salami
- Jerky with artificial preservatives
- Canned meats

What really convinced me to change was research showing that even small amounts matter. The Harvard School of Public Health found that consuming just one serving of processed meat per day (about one hot dog or two slices of deli meat) increased inflammatory markers significantly.

The good news? High-quality, minimally processed meats from grass-fed, pasture-raised animals have anti-inflammatory properties. The key is choosing meats that are raised properly and processed minimally.

Reading labels like a detective (because that's what it takes)

Learning to read food labels properly was like learning a new language—one that food manufacturers desperately don't want you to understand. They've mastered the art of making inflammatory ingredients sound benign or even healthy.

The label tricks that fooled me for years:

- "Natural flavors" can include over 100 different chemical compounds, many of which are inflammatory. There's nothing requiring these flavors to actually be derived from natural sources in a natural way.

- "Made with whole grains" often means the product contains some whole grains mixed with refined flours, sugars, and inflammatory oils. The amount of whole grains might be minimal.

- "No trans fats" can legally be used if the product contains less than 0.5 grams per serving. But if you eat multiple servings or if the serving size is unrealistically small, you're still getting trans fats.

- "Heart-healthy" usually means the product is low in saturated fat but says nothing about inflammatory ingredients, sugar content, or overall nutritional quality.

The ingredient red flags I learned to spot:

- Anything ending in "-ose" (dextrose, maltose, sucrose) is sugar, even if it's not listed as sugar.
- Inflammatory oils hiding under names like "vegetable oil," "soybean oil," or even "natural oil blend."
- Preservatives like BHT, BHA, TBHQ, and sodium benzoate that have been linked to inflammatory responses.
- Artificial colors (Red 40, Yellow 5, Blue 1) that can trigger inflammatory reactions, especially in sensitive individuals.
- Carrageenan, a thickener derived from seaweed that can cause intestinal inflammation.
- High-fructose corn syrup, which is even more inflammatory than regular sugar.

My label-reading strategy now:

If I can't pronounce an ingredient or don't know what it is, I research it before buying the product.

I look for products with five ingredients or fewer, all of which I recognize as actual food.

I check the ingredient list, not just the marketing claims on the front of the package.

I pay attention to serving sizes, which are often unrealistically small to make the nutrition facts look better.

I look for third-party certifications like organic, grass-fed, or non-GMO when relevant.

The sneaky ingredients with names you can't pronounce

The food industry has become incredibly sophisticated at disguising inflammatory ingredients behind scientific-sounding names that most people don't recognize. It's like they're speaking in code, and the code is designed to hide ingredients that could trigger inflammatory responses.

The inflammatory additives hiding in plain sight:

- Monosodium glutamate (MSG) and its disguises: MSG is a known inflammatory trigger for many people, causing headaches, joint pain, and digestive issues. But it often hides under names like "yeast extract," "hydrolyzed protein," "autolyzed yeast," "natural flavoring," and "protein isolate."

- Carrageenan: This seaweed-derived thickener is used in many "healthy" products like organic milk, yogurt, and plant-based milk alternatives. Research from the University of Illinois shows that carrageenan can cause intestinal inflammation and has been linked to inflammatory bowel conditions.

- Polysorbate 80: An emulsifier found in many processed foods, ice cream, and supplements. Studies suggest it can disrupt gut bacteria and increase intestinal permeability, contributing to systemic inflammation.

- Sodium benzoate: A preservative that can form benzene (a carcinogen) when combined with vitamin C. It's been linked to hyperactivity in children and inflammatory responses in sensitive individuals.

- Artificial sweeteners: Aspartame, sucralose, and acesulfame potassium may not contain calories, but research suggests they can disrupt gut bacteria and trigger inflammatory responses. A study in Nature found that artificial sweeteners can promote glucose intolerance and inflammation.

- Titanium dioxide: Used as a whitening agent in many foods, from candy to salad dressings. The European Food Safety Authority recently banned it due to concerns about inflammatory effects and potential DNA damage.

How to spot inflammation triggers hiding in plain sight

After years of label reading and research, I've developed a system for quickly identifying potentially inflammatory foods, even when the marketing makes them sound healthy.

Red flag foods disguised as healthy options:

- Granola and granola bars: Often loaded with inflammatory oils, high amounts of sugar, and artificial preservatives. Even "natural" versions frequently contain inflammatory ingredients.

- Veggie chips: Usually just regular potato chips made with vegetable powder and inflammatory oils. The vegetable content is minimal, and the inflammatory oil content is maximal.

- Protein bars: Many contain inflammatory oils, artificial sweeteners, and enough sugar to spike your blood glucose significantly.

- Flavored yogurt: Can contain more sugar than ice cream, plus artificial flavors, colors, and thickeners that may trigger inflammatory responses.

- Whole grain breakfast cereals: Often contain more sugar than actual whole grains, plus inflammatory preservatives and artificial vitamins that may not be well-absorbed.

- Plant-based meat alternatives: While the concept is good, many are highly processed with inflammatory oils, artificial flavors, and preservatives. Some are more inflammatory than the meat they're replacing.

- Energy drinks and sports drinks: Loaded with inflammatory sweeteners, artificial colors, and often caffeine levels that can trigger stress responses and inflammation.

The shopping strategy that changed everything for me:

I shop the perimeter of the store first—fresh produce, meat, fish, and dairy. These whole foods don't need ingredient lists because they are the ingredient.

When I do buy packaged foods, I spend more time reading the ingredient list than looking at the nutrition facts panel.

I've learned to be suspicious of health claims on packaging. The more health claims a product makes, the more likely it is to be highly processed.

I look for foods with short ingredient lists where I recognize every ingredient as actual food.

I pay attention to how I feel after eating certain foods, regardless of whether they're marketed as healthy.

The transformation in my shopping cart was dramatic. Instead of aisles full of boxes and bags, I started filling my cart with fresh vegetables, quality proteins, healthy fats, and minimal amounts of carefully chosen packaged foods.

But here's what surprised me most: once I stopped eating inflammatory foods regularly, my taste buds completely recalibrated. Foods I used to think were bland became flavorful. Products I used to crave started tasting artificial and overly sweet or salty.

The grocery store went from being a place of confusion and temptation to being a place where I could make informed choices that supported my health rather than undermining it. The middle aisles didn't disappear, but they stopped calling my name.

Understanding which foods were betraying my health was the first step toward reclaiming it. Once you know what to look for, you can't unsee it. And once you experience how much better you feel without inflammatory foods, you won't want to go back to eating them regularly.

The foods that betrayed us did so gradually, quietly, and with excellent marketing. But now that we know better, we can do better. And that's exactly what we're going to explore next—the foods that heal instead of harm.

CHAPTER FOUR: The Kitchen Revolution—How to Cook Without Adding Fuel to The Fire

The day I threw out my deep fryer (and why you might want to consider it)

I'll never forget standing in my kitchen, holding my beloved deep fryer and having what I can only describe as a moment of clarity. This thing had been my go-to for Sunday family dinners, weekend entertaining, and those times when I wanted to make something "special." But as I learned more about how cooking methods affect inflammation, I realized my trusty deep fryer was basically an inflammation-generating machine.

It wasn't an easy decision. I'm not one of those people who can just toss out kitchen equipment without a pang of regret. This fryer had made countless batches of crispy chicken, golden french fries, and those amazing onion rings that everyone raved about at parties. But here's what I'd learned that changed everything: deep frying doesn't just add calories—it creates inflammatory compounds that your body has to deal with long after the meal is over.

Research from Mount Sinai School of Medicine shows that deep frying creates advanced glycation end products (AGEs) at levels up to 150 times higher than gentler cooking methods. These AGEs aren't just scary-sounding compounds—they're literally inflammatory toxins that accumulate in your tissues and trigger chronic inflammatory responses.

The study that really opened my eyes was published in the Journal of the American Dietetic Association. Researchers compared inflammatory markers in people who ate the same foods prepared different ways. Those eating deep-fried foods had significantly higher levels of C-reactive protein, interleukin-6, and other inflammatory markers within just four hours of eating. The inflammation lasted for up to 8 hours after the meal.

But here's what really got me: it wasn't just about the oil (though that matters too). It was about what happens to food when you subject it to those extremely high temperatures. Proteins become denatured in inflammatory ways, natural antioxidants get destroyed, and new compounds form that your body recognizes as foreign invaders.

So yes, I threw out my deep fryer. And you know what? I don't miss it. Not because I don't miss crispy foods (I definitely do), but because I've learned ways to get that satisfying crunch and flavor without creating inflammatory havoc in my body.

Cooking methods that were making me sicker without knowing it

The deep fryer was just the beginning. As I dove deeper into the research on cooking methods and inflammation, I realized that several of my favorite cooking techniques were actually working against my health goals.

High-Heat Grilling and Charring: The Backyard Trap

I used to pride myself on those perfect grill marks and that slightly charred flavor that comes from high-heat grilling. Turns out, those beautiful char marks are actually concentrations of inflammatory compounds called heterocyclic amines (HCAs) and polycyclic aromatic hydrocarbons (PAHs).

Research from the National Cancer Institute shows that these compounds form when amino acids, sugars, and creatine react at high temperatures. The darker the char, the higher the concentration of inflammatory compounds. People who regularly consume charred meats have significantly higher inflammatory markers and increased risk of chronic diseases.

The temperature matters enormously. Cooking at temperatures above 300°F (150°C) dramatically increases inflammatory compound formation. Most grilling happens at 400-500°F (200-260°C), which is right in the danger zone.

Dry Roasting at High Temperatures: The Oven Mistake

This one surprised me because roasting seems so healthy compared to frying. But roasting at high temperatures (above 350°F/175°C) creates similar problems to grilling. The Maillard reaction that creates those appealing brown, crispy surfaces also creates inflammatory AGEs.

A study published in Food Chemistry found that vegetables roasted at high temperatures lost up to 90% of their antioxidant content while simultaneously generating inflammatory compounds. The very foods I thought were my healthiest choices were being transformed into inflammatory triggers by how I was cooking them.

The Microwave Dilemma: Convenience with Consequences

Now, this is where I'm going to lose some of you, and I get it. Microwaves are convenient, fast, and seem harmless. But the research on microwave cooking and inflammation is concerning enough that I felt I had to address it.

Microwave cooking works by agitating water molecules at extremely high frequencies—2.45 billion times per second. This creates what researchers call "molecular friction" that generates heat from the inside out. While this cooks food quickly, it also disrupts molecular structures in ways that other cooking methods don't.

Studies from Stanford University and the University of Minnesota found that microwaving can reduce antioxidant activity in foods by 60-90%. But more concerning is research showing that microwaved foods can create new compounds that aren't present in the original food or in the same food cooked by other methods.

A study published in the Journal of Food Science found that people who regularly consumed microwaved foods had higher levels of inflammatory markers compared to those eating the same foods prepared by conventional cooking methods. The researchers hypothesized that the unique molecular changes caused by microwave radiation created compounds that triggered inflammatory responses.

The Hidden Problem with Non-Stick Cookware

This was another eye-opener for me. Those convenient non-stick pans that make cleanup so easy? They release perfluorinated compounds (PFCs) when heated, especially at high temperatures. These compounds accumulate in your body and have been linked to increased inflammation and various health issues.

Research from the Environmental Protection Agency shows that PFC exposure is associated with elevated inflammatory markers and increased risk of autoimmune conditions. The compounds don't break down in the body and can accumulate over years of exposure.

The gentle art of anti-inflammatory cooking

Once I understood what cooking methods were creating inflammation, I needed to figure out what cooking methods actually supported health. This is where the real kitchen revolution began—discovering that anti-inflammatory cooking isn't about sacrifice, it's about technique.

Water-Based Cooking: Your New Best Friend

Steaming, poaching, braising, and gentle simmering became my go-to methods. These techniques cook food at temperatures below 212°F (100°C), which prevents the formation of inflammatory compounds while preserving and even enhancing the nutritional content of foods.

Research from the University of California Davis found that steamed vegetables retained 95% of their antioxidant content compared to only 45% when roasted at high heat. Steaming also makes nutrients more bioavailable—your body can actually absorb more of the good stuff.

Poaching is incredible for proteins. Fish, chicken, and even eggs cooked this way retain their anti-inflammatory omega-3 fatty acids and don't form any harmful compounds. The gentle heat preserves the protein structure while making it easily digestible.

Low-Temperature Roasting: The Sweet Spot

I didn't give up roasting entirely—I just changed my approach. Roasting at 275-325°F (135-165°C) gives you many of the flavors you love without creating significant inflammatory compounds. It takes a bit longer, but the results are worth it.

This temperature range allows the natural sugars in vegetables to caramelize slowly, creating complex flavors without the inflammatory AGEs that form at higher temperatures. Proteins cooked this way stay tender and retain their beneficial compounds.

Pressure Cooking: The Game Changer

My pressure cooker (specifically an Instant Pot) became one of my most valuable kitchen tools. Pressure cooking uses moist heat at temperatures around 250°F (120°C), which is hot enough to cook food quickly but not hot enough to create significant inflammatory compounds.

Research shows that pressure cooking actually increases the antioxidant content of many foods while reducing cooking time by 50-70%. It's particularly excellent for legumes, which become more digestible and anti-inflammatory when pressure cooked.

Raw Preparation: Not Just Salads

I started incorporating more raw foods, not because I became a raw food fanatic, but because I realized that some foods are most anti-inflammatory when uncooked. Raw garlic, for example, contains allicin compounds that are destroyed by heat but are powerfully anti-inflammatory when consumed raw.

Raw preparation also includes techniques like marinating, which can pre-digest proteins and add anti-inflammatory herbs and spices. A simple marinade with olive oil, lemon juice, and herbs like rosemary or thyme can actually make foods more anti-inflammatory than they would be plain.

Fermentation: Ancient Wisdom, Modern Science

Fermented foods became a regular part of my cooking routine. Fermentation not only preserves food but actually creates new anti-inflammatory compounds while making nutrients more bioavailable.

Research from Stanford University shows that people who regularly consume fermented foods have lower inflammatory markers and improved immune function. The beneficial bacteria in fermented foods help regulate inflammatory responses throughout the body.

Kitchen tools that became my best friends

Changing how I cooked meant investing in some new kitchen tools, but these weren't expensive gadgets—they were simple, effective tools that made anti-inflammatory cooking easier and more enjoyable.

Stainless Steel and Cast Iron: The Safe Choices

I replaced all my non-stick cookware with stainless steel and well-seasoned cast iron. Yes, there's a learning curve with these materials, but once you understand how to use them properly, they're actually superior for cooking.

Stainless steel doesn't release any compounds into your food, and it heats evenly when you preheat it properly. Cast iron adds a small amount of bioavailable iron to your food, which can be beneficial, especially for people with iron deficiency.

The key with both is proper preheating and using adequate fat (like olive oil or avocado oil) to prevent sticking. Once you get the technique down, cleanup is actually easier than you'd expect.

Bamboo Steamer: Simple and Effective

A bamboo steamer became my secret weapon for vegetables. It sits right over a pot of simmering water and cooks vegetables perfectly while preserving their nutrients and natural flavors. Plus, it looks beautiful on the table if you want to serve directly from it.

Quality Knife Set: Worth the Investment

Good knives make all the difference when you're preparing more fresh foods. You don't need a whole block of knives—just a few high-quality ones that hold their edge. Sharp knives make prep work faster and more enjoyable, which means you're more likely to actually cook this way consistently.

Glass Storage Containers: Avoiding Plastic

I switched all my food storage to glass containers with secure lids. Plastic containers can leach compounds into your food, especially when heated or when storing acidic foods. Glass is completely inert and doesn't add anything unwanted to your carefully prepared anti-inflammatory meals.

Instant Pot or Pressure Cooker: The Time Saver

This was probably my best purchase. The Instant Pot makes it possible to prepare anti-inflammatory meals quickly, which is crucial for busy schedules. It's perfect for cooking beans, making bone broth, preparing grains, and even steaming vegetables.

Transforming your favorite recipes (yes, even grandma's casserole)

This was the part I was most worried about. I didn't want to give up all the foods I loved—I wanted to find ways to make them work with my new understanding of anti-inflammatory cooking.

The Fried Chicken Revolution

Instead of deep frying, I learned to make incredibly crispy "fried" chicken using a technique called steam-frying. You start by steaming the chicken until it's cooked through, then finish it in a hot pan with a small amount of healthy oil to crisp the outside. You get the crispy texture without the inflammatory compounds.

For the coating, I replaced white flour with almond flour or coconut flour mixed with anti-inflammatory spices like turmeric, paprika, and garlic powder. The result is actually more flavorful than traditional fried chicken.

Grandma's Casserole Gets a Makeover

Most casseroles can be adapted by changing the cooking temperature and a few ingredients. Instead of baking at 375°F, I cook at 325°F for a slightly longer time. I replace inflammatory ingredients like processed cheese with real cheese, and processed meats with fresh, high-quality proteins.

The key is understanding what makes each dish special and finding anti-inflammatory ways to achieve those same flavors and textures. Grandma's casserole was special because it was comforting and brought the family together—those qualities don't depend on inflammatory cooking methods.

Pizza Night Saved

Pizza was non-negotiable in our house, so I had to figure out how to make it work. I make the dough with organic flour and let it rise slowly for better digestibility. I use a pizza stone in the oven at a moderate temperature (around 450°F) rather than the blazing hot temperatures that create inflammatory compounds.

For toppings, I load up on anti-inflammatory vegetables and use high-quality cheese and meats. The result is pizza that tastes even better than takeout and doesn't leave me feeling inflamed and sluggish.

Meal prep strategies that actually work for real life

Anti-inflammatory cooking works best when you're not stressed about what to make for dinner every night. These meal prep strategies have made all the difference in making this approach sustainable.

Batch Cooking Proteins

Every Sunday, I cook several proteins using anti-inflammatory methods. I might poach a whole chicken, steam fish fillets, and slow-cook some grass-fed beef. Having these ready makes it easy to throw together quick meals during the week.

Pre-Prepped Vegetables

I wash, chop, and steam large batches of vegetables on prep day. Steamed vegetables keep well in the refrigerator and can be quickly reheated or added to salads throughout the week.

Make-Ahead Marinades

I prepare several different marinades in small containers. During the week, I can quickly marinate proteins for 30 minutes before cooking, which adds flavor and anti-inflammatory compounds without much effort.

One-Pot Wonders

I developed a repertoire of one-pot meals that can be made in my pressure cooker or on the stovetop. These meals combine proteins, vegetables, and healthy fats in one dish, making both cooking and cleanup simple.

Freezer-Friendly Options

Some anti-inflammatory dishes freeze beautifully. I make large batches of things like vegetable soups, stews, and marinara sauce, then freeze them in individual portions. Having these on hand prevents the temptation to order inflammatory takeout on busy nights.

Why your microwave might not be your friend

I saved this for last because I know it's controversial. Microwaves are so convenient that suggesting you might want to reconsider using them feels almost unreasonable. But the research is concerning enough that I felt I had to address it honestly.

The Molecular Changes

Microwave radiation creates molecular changes in food that don't occur with other cooking methods. While these changes don't make food radioactive or immediately dangerous, they do appear to affect how your body responds to the food.

A study published in Food Chemistry found that microwaved foods triggered different inflammatory responses compared to the same foods cooked conventionally. The researchers noted that the unique molecular alterations caused by microwave radiation created compounds that the immune system didn't recognize as normal food components.

The Nutrient Loss

Multiple studies have shown that microwaving reduces the antioxidant content of foods more than other cooking methods. Since antioxidants are crucial for fighting inflammation, this nutrient loss undermines one of the main reasons for eating anti-inflammatory foods in the first place.

Practical Alternatives

If you're not ready to give up your microwave entirely, consider using it only for reheating rather than actual cooking. For quick meals, a toaster oven set to a moderate temperature often works just as fast and doesn't create the same molecular changes.

Steaming is actually faster than microwaving for many vegetables, and it preserves more nutrients while avoiding any potential inflammatory compounds.

The Container Issue

Even if you continue using your microwave, avoid heating food in plastic containers. The microwave radiation can cause plastic to release compounds into your food. Use glass or ceramic containers instead.

Look, I'm not telling you that using a microwave occasionally is going to ruin your health. But if you're serious about reducing inflammation, it's worth considering whether the convenience is worth the potential downsides. For me, learning alternative quick-cooking methods was easier than I expected and actually improved the taste and nutritional quality of my food.

The kitchen revolution isn't about making cooking harder—it's about making it more intentional. Once you understand how different cooking methods affect inflammation, you can make informed choices that support your health goals while still enjoying delicious, satisfying food.

Your kitchen can be a pharmacy or a place that creates inflammation. The choice is literally in your hands.

CHAPTER FIVE: The Healing Foods—Nature's Anti-Inflammatory Pharmacy

The grocery list that changed my life

I'll never forget the first time I walked into the grocery store with my new anti-inflammatory shopping list. I felt like I was seeing the place with completely different eyes. Foods I'd walked past for years suddenly looked like medicine bottles. The produce section became a pharmacy. The spice aisle transformed into a collection of healing compounds that had been hiding in plain sight.

That first shopping trip took me twice as long as usual because I kept stopping to read labels and marvel at how much healing potential was sitting right there on the shelves. I'd been searching for solutions in doctor's offices and supplement stores while the most powerful anti-inflammatory tools were available at any grocery store for the price of a prescription co-pay.

Six months later, my inflammatory markers had dropped by 60%. My joint pain was virtually gone. My energy levels were steady throughout the day. And my grocery bill? Actually lower than before, because I wasn't buying expensive processed foods, energy drinks, or takeout as often.

Here's what nobody tells you about anti-inflammatory eating: it's not about restriction or deprivation. It's about abundance. You'll be adding so many delicious, satisfying foods to your life that you won't miss the inflammatory ones. Your taste buds will actually change, and foods that used to seem bland will burst with flavor once your palate adjusts.

My go-to anti-inflammatory grocery list:

- Proteins that heal: Wild-caught salmon, sardines, anchovies, mackerel, pasture-raised eggs, grass-fed beef (in moderation), organic chicken, hemp hearts, walnuts, and legumes

- Vegetables that fight fire: Dark leafy greens, broccoli, Brussels sprouts, cauliflower, bell peppers, tomatoes, sweet potatoes, beets, carrots, and onions

- Fruits that pack a punch: Blueberries, cherries, pomegranates, oranges, apples, avocados, and berries of all kinds

- Fats that heal: Extra virgin olive oil, avocado oil, coconut oil, nuts, seeds, and olives

- Spices that work like medicine: Turmeric, ginger, garlic, cinnamon, oregano, basil, and rosemary

- Whole grains that support: Steel-cut oats, quinoa, brown rice, and buckwheat

The beauty of this list is its flexibility. You don't need to eat every single item every day. You're not following a rigid meal plan or counting anything. You're simply choosing from a variety of foods that actively work to reduce inflammation in your body.

Superfoods that actually live up to the hype

I used to roll my eyes at the term "superfood." It seemed like marketing hype designed to sell expensive, exotic ingredients that would probably end up forgotten in the back of my pantry. But when I started researching the anti-inflammatory properties of certain foods, I realized that some of them really do deserve special recognition.

Blueberries: The Antioxidant Powerhouse

Research from Tufts University found that blueberries have one of the highest antioxidant capacities of any food. Just one cup contains more than 13,000 antioxidant units. But here's what's really impressive: a study published in the Journal of Nutrition found that eating just one cup of blueberries daily for eight weeks reduced inflammatory markers by 18% and improved insulin sensitivity.

The anthocyanins in blueberries—the compounds that give them their deep blue color—are particularly potent anti-inflammatory agents. Research shows they can cross the blood-brain barrier and accumulate in brain regions responsible for memory and learning, potentially protecting against cognitive decline.

Fatty Fish: Swimming in Anti-Inflammatory Gold

If there's one food that could single-handedly transform your inflammatory status, it's fatty fish rich in omega-3 fatty acids. The research is so compelling that the American Heart Association recommends eating fatty fish at least twice a week specifically for its anti-inflammatory benefits.

A landmark study published in the New England Journal of Medicine followed over 11,000 people for 3.5 years and found that those with the highest blood levels of omega-3s had a 25% lower risk of heart attack and a 20% lower risk of coronary heart disease death.

But the benefits go way beyond heart health. Research from Harvard Medical School shows that omega-3s from fish can reduce joint pain and stiffness in people with rheumatoid arthritis by up to 30%. A study in the journal Brain Research found that omega-3s can reduce neuroinflammation and may help prevent age-related cognitive decline.

Leafy Greens: The Unsung Heroes

Spinach, kale, arugula, Swiss chard—these aren't just trendy health foods, they're anti-inflammatory powerhouses. Research from Rush University found that people who ate just one serving of leafy greens daily had brains that were 11 years younger than those who rarely ate them.

Leafy greens are loaded with vitamin K, which plays a crucial role in regulating inflammatory responses. They're also rich in nitrates, which convert to nitric oxide in the body and help reduce inflammation in blood vessels. A study published in Nitric Oxide journal found that dietary nitrates from leafy greens could reduce inflammatory markers by up to 15% within just two weeks.

Turmeric: The Golden Healer

Curcumin, the active compound in turmeric, has been used medicinally for over 4,000 years, and modern research is proving why. Over 3,000 studies have been published on curcumin's effects, with many showing it to be as effective as some pharmaceutical anti-inflammatory drugs—without the side effects.

A study published in the Journal of Medicinal Food found that curcumin was as effective as ibuprofen for reducing pain and improving function in people with knee osteoarthritis. Another study in the journal Oncogene found that curcumin was more effective than aspirin and ibuprofen at inhibiting inflammatory enzyme activity.

The key with turmeric is absorption. Curcumin is poorly absorbed on its own, but combining it with black pepper (which contains piperine) can increase absorption by up to 2,000%. Adding a little fat also helps, since curcumin is fat-soluble.

Why some fish are liquid gold for your joints

Not all fish are created equal when it comes to anti-inflammatory benefits. The fish that provide the most powerful anti-inflammatory effects are those highest in omega-3 fatty acids, particularly EPA (eicosapentaenoic acid) and DHA (docosahexaenoic acid).

The omega-3 champions:

- Wild-caught salmon contains about 1,500mg of omega-3s per 3.5-ounce serving. But here's why wild-caught matters: farmed salmon often has higher levels of inflammatory omega-6 fatty acids and lower levels of beneficial omega-3s due to their grain-based diet.

- Sardines are omega-3 superstars, with about 1,400mg per serving, plus they're low in mercury and high in calcium. They're also one of the most sustainable fish options.

- Mackerel provides about 1,100mg of omega-3s per serving and is rich in vitamin D, which also has anti-inflammatory properties.

- Anchovies contain about 950mg of omega-3s per serving and are incredibly versatile—you can add them to salads, pasta dishes, or pizza for a boost of flavor and nutrition.

Research from the University of Pittsburgh found that people who consumed the equivalent of 2-3 servings of fatty fish per week had 29% lower levels of inflammatory markers compared to those who rarely ate fish. The omega-3s in these fish actually get incorporated into cell membranes throughout your body, where they produce anti-inflammatory compounds called resolvins and protectins.

The joint connection:

For joint health specifically, the research on fish omega-3s is remarkable. A study published in Arthritis & Rheumatism followed people with rheumatoid arthritis for 24 weeks and found that those taking fish oil supplements (equivalent to eating 3-4 servings of fatty fish per week) reduced their joint pain by 42% and morning stiffness by 34%.

But you don't need arthritis to benefit. Research shows that omega-3s from fish can reduce exercise-induced joint inflammation, speed recovery from workouts, and even help prevent age-related joint degeneration.

The vegetables that pack the biggest anti-inflammatory punch

While all vegetables provide some anti-inflammatory benefits, certain ones are particularly powerful. These are the vegetables I prioritize when I'm grocery shopping, and they're the ones that have the strongest research backing for reducing systemic inflammation.

Cruciferous Vegetables: The Detox Champions

Broccoli, cauliflower, Brussels sprouts, kale, and cabbage all contain compounds called glucosinolates, which break down into powerful anti-inflammatory substances like sulforaphane. Research from Johns Hopkins found that sulforaphane can reduce inflammatory markers by up to 20% and may help protect against cancer.

A study published in Arthritis & Rheumatism found that people who ate the most cruciferous vegetables had 25% lower levels of inflammatory markers compared to those who ate the least. The researchers noted that just one serving per day made a measurable difference.

Bell Peppers: Vitamin C Powerhouses

Red bell peppers contain more vitamin C than oranges—about 190mg per cup compared to 70mg in an orange. Vitamin C is a potent antioxidant that helps neutralize free radicals and reduce inflammatory damage. Research shows that people with higher vitamin C levels have lower levels of C-reactive protein, a key inflammatory marker.

Tomatoes: Lycopene Leaders

Tomatoes are rich in lycopene, a carotenoid that gives them their red color and provides powerful anti-inflammatory effects. Interestingly, cooked tomatoes contain more bioavailable lycopene than raw ones, so tomato sauce, paste, and soup are all excellent choices.

A study published in the American Journal of Clinical Nutrition found that people with the highest lycopene levels had 34% lower levels of inflammatory markers compared to those with the lowest levels.

Sweet Potatoes: Beta-Carotene Builders

Sweet potatoes are loaded with beta-carotene, which converts to vitamin A in the body. Vitamin A plays crucial roles in immune function and inflammation regulation. Research shows that adequate vitamin A intake can help prevent the overproduction of inflammatory cytokines.

Beets: Nitric Oxide Boosters

Beets are rich in nitrates, which convert to nitric oxide in the body. Nitric oxide helps relax blood vessels and reduce vascular inflammation. A study published in the journal Nutrients found that drinking beet juice for just one week reduced inflammatory markers and improved blood vessel function.

Spices that do more than just taste good

This is where anti-inflammatory eating gets really exciting. Spices aren't just about adding flavor—they're concentrated sources of anti-inflammatory compounds that can dramatically enhance the healing power of your meals.

Turmeric: The Anti-Inflammatory Superstar

We touched on this earlier, but turmeric deserves deeper discussion. Curcumin, its active compound, inhibits multiple inflammatory pathways simultaneously. Research from UCLA found that curcumin supplements reduced inflammatory markers by 58% in healthy adults within just eight weeks.

The key is using it regularly and enhancing absorption with black pepper and fat. I add turmeric to everything—scrambled eggs, roasted vegetables, soups, and smoothies.

Ginger: The Digestive Healer

Ginger contains compounds called gingerols that have potent anti-inflammatory effects. Research published in the Journal of Medicinal Food found that ginger extract reduced inflammatory markers by 25% in people with osteoarthritis.

Ginger is particularly effective for reducing digestive inflammation. A study in the World Journal of Gastroenterology found that ginger could reduce inflammation in the digestive tract and help heal intestinal damage.

Garlic: The Immune Booster

Garlic contains sulfur compounds that have both anti-inflammatory and antimicrobial properties. Research shows that aged garlic extract can reduce inflammatory markers and support immune function. A study published in Clinical Nutrition found that garlic supplements reduced C-reactive protein levels by 10% in just 12 weeks.

Cinnamon: The Blood Sugar Stabilizer

Cinnamon doesn't just taste great—it helps stabilize blood sugar levels, which reduces inflammatory spikes caused by glucose fluctuations. Research published in Diabetes Care found that just half a teaspoon of cinnamon daily could reduce inflammatory markers in people with type 2 diabetes.

Oregano: The Antioxidant Champion

Oregano has one of the highest antioxidant activities of any herb. It contains compounds like rosmarinic acid and thymol that have powerful anti-inflammatory effects. Research shows that oregano extract can inhibit inflammatory enzyme activity as effectively as some prescription anti-inflammatory drugs.

The fat fears we need to forget

For decades, we've been told that fat makes us fat and clogs our arteries. But research now shows that the right kinds of fats are not only healthy—they're essential for reducing inflammation and supporting overall health.

The omega-3 revolution:

The most important anti-inflammatory fats are omega-3 fatty acids, particularly EPA and DHA from fish and ALA from plant sources like walnuts, flaxseeds, and chia seeds. These fats actually get incorporated into cell membranes throughout your body, where they produce anti-inflammatory compounds and help regulate immune responses.

Research from Harvard Medical School found that people with the highest omega-3 levels had 23% lower levels of inflammatory markers compared to those with the lowest levels. The anti-inflammatory effects were dose-dependent, meaning more omega-3s provided greater benefits.

Monounsaturated fats: The Mediterranean secret

Olive oil, avocados, nuts, and seeds are rich in monounsaturated fats that have been shown to reduce inflammation. The Mediterranean diet, which is high in these fats, has been extensively studied for its anti-inflammatory effects.

Extra virgin olive oil contains compounds called oleocanthal and oleuropein that have anti-inflammatory effects similar to ibuprofen. Research published in Nature found that consuming about 3.5 tablespoons of extra virgin olive oil provides anti-inflammatory effects comparable to 10% of the adult dose of ibuprofen.

Saturated fat: It's complicated

The research on saturated fat and inflammation is more nuanced than we once thought. While processed meats and fried foods high in saturated fat do increase inflammation, natural sources like coconut oil, grass-fed butter, and fatty cuts of pasture-raised meat may actually have neutral or even anti-inflammatory effects when consumed in moderation as part of an overall anti-inflammatory diet.

A study published in the American Journal of Clinical Nutrition found that the source and quality of saturated fat mattered more than the quantity. Saturated fat from processed foods increased inflammation, while saturated fat from whole food sources did not.

The fats to avoid:

Trans fats and highly processed vegetable oils (corn, soybean, sunflower, safflower) are the real inflammatory culprits. These fats are high in omega-6 fatty acids, which promote inflammation when consumed in excess. The typical Western diet has an omega-6 to omega-3 ratio of about 20:1, when it should be closer to 4:1 for optimal health.

Building meals that heal instead of harm

Now that you know which individual foods fight inflammation, let's talk about how to combine them into meals that are both delicious and healing. The key is thinking about every meal as an opportunity to either support your body's anti-inflammatory processes or work against them.

The anti-inflammatory plate:

- Half your plate: Colorful vegetables, with an emphasis on dark leafy greens, cruciferous vegetables, and bright-colored options like bell peppers and tomatoes

- One quarter: High-quality protein, particularly fatty fish 2-3 times per week, with other options including pasture-raised poultry, grass-fed meat, legumes, or eggs

- One quarter: Complex carbohydrates like sweet potatoes, quinoa, brown rice, or other whole grains

- Healthy fats: A drizzle of extra virgin olive oil, half an avocado, a handful of nuts or seeds, or olives

- Herbs and spices: Liberal use of turmeric, ginger, garlic, and other anti-inflammatory seasonings

Meal combinations that maximize benefits:

- Salmon with turmeric and black pepper - The omega-3s in salmon combined with curcumin create a powerful anti-inflammatory synergy

- Spinach salad with walnuts and olive oil - The omega-3s in walnuts, vitamin K in spinach, and polyphenols in olive oil work together to reduce inflammation

- Blueberry and flaxseed smoothie - Antioxidants from blueberries plus omega-3s from flaxseeds provide complementary anti-inflammatory effects

- Roasted vegetables with garlic and rosemary - The antioxidants in colorful vegetables are enhanced by the anti-inflammatory compounds in herbs

Timing matters too:

Research shows that eating anti-inflammatory foods consistently throughout the day helps maintain steady levels of beneficial compounds in your bloodstream. Rather than trying to get all your anti-inflammatory foods in one meal, spread them throughout the day.

Smart supplementation (when food isn't enough)

While I always recommend getting nutrients from food first, there are times when targeted supplementation can enhance your anti-inflammatory efforts. This is especially true if you're dealing with significant inflammatory conditions or have dietary restrictions that make it difficult to get optimal amounts of certain nutrients from food alone.

The supplements with the strongest research backing:

- Omega-3 fish oil: If you're not eating 2-3 servings of fatty fish per week, a high-quality fish oil supplement can help bridge the gap. Look for one that provides at least 1,000mg of combined EPA and DHA daily. Research shows that this amount can reduce inflammatory markers by 10-15% within 8-12 weeks.

- Curcumin: While you can get curcumin from turmeric, therapeutic doses often require supplementation. Look for curcumin with enhanced absorption (paired with piperine or in a liposomal form). Studies show that 500-1,000mg daily can significantly reduce inflammatory markers.

- Vitamin D: Most people are deficient in vitamin D, which plays crucial roles in immune function and inflammation regulation. Research shows that people with vitamin D deficiency have higher levels of inflammatory markers. The optimal blood level is 30-50 ng/mL, which often requires 1,000-4,000 IU of supplementation daily.

- Magnesium: This mineral is involved in over 300 enzymatic reactions and helps regulate inflammatory responses. Research shows that magnesium deficiency is associated with higher levels of inflammatory markers. Most people benefit from 200-400mg daily.

- Probiotics: Since gut health is so closely linked to systemic inflammation, a high-quality probiotic can help support anti-inflammatory efforts. Look for one with multiple strains and at least 10 billion CFU.

Quality matters:

Not all supplements are created equal. Look for third-party tested products from reputable companies. For fish oil, choose brands that test for heavy metals and provide certificates of analysis. For curcumin, choose forms with enhanced bioavailability.

Work with a healthcare provider:

Before starting any supplement regimen, especially if you're taking medications or dealing with chronic health conditions, work with a healthcare provider who understands both conventional medicine and nutritional approaches.

Remember: supplements supplement, they don't replace:

Even the best supplements can't make up for a poor diet. Think of them as insurance or enhancement for an already solid anti-inflammatory eating plan, not as a way to cancel out inflammatory food choices.

The goal is to create a comprehensive approach where food is your primary medicine and supplements provide targeted support where needed. When you combine anti-inflammatory foods with smart supplementation and the lifestyle factors we'll discuss in later chapters, you create a powerful system for reducing chronic inflammation and supporting optimal health.

Your body has an incredible capacity for healing when you give it the right tools. Every meal is an opportunity to provide those tools, and every bite is a choice to either support inflammation or fight it. Choose wisely, and your body will thank you with better energy, less pain, improved mood, and enhanced overall vitality.

CHAPTER SIX: Your Second Brain—Why Gut Health Changes Everything

The gut-inflammation connection nobody talks about enough

I'll never forget the moment I realized my gut was running the show. I was sitting in a functional medicine doctor's office, complaining about brain fog, joint pain, and crushing afternoon fatigue, when she asked me something no other doctor had ever asked: "Tell me about your digestion."

"My digestion? What does that have to do with my energy and joint pain?"

Her response changed everything: "Your gut produces more neurotransmitters than your brain. It houses 70% of your immune system. And if it's inflamed, the rest of your body will be too."

Wait, what?

Turns out, your digestive system isn't just about breaking down food—it's the command center for your entire inflammatory response. The scientific term for this is the "gut-brain axis," but I like to think of your gut as your second brain because that's essentially what it is.

Here's what blew my mind: your intestinal tract contains over 500 million neurons—more than your spinal cord. It produces 90% of your body's serotonin, the neurotransmitter responsible for mood regulation. It manufactures more than 30 different neurotransmitters. And it's in constant communication with your actual brain through the vagus nerve, sending signals that affect everything from your mood to your immune response.

But here's the kicker—when your gut is inflamed, it becomes like a broken telephone line. The signals get distorted, inflammation spreads throughout your body, and suddenly you're dealing with symptoms that seem completely unrelated to digestion.

Research from Harvard Medical School shows that people with inflammatory bowel conditions have significantly higher rates of depression, anxiety, and cognitive dysfunction—not because they're sad about being sick, but because gut inflammation directly affects brain function. A groundbreaking study published in

Nature Microbiology found that inflammatory changes in the gut can trigger neuroinflammation within 24 hours.

The Mayo Clinic published research showing that 84% of people with irritable bowel syndrome also struggle with anxiety or depression. Johns Hopkins found that people with gut inflammation had measurably different brain activity patterns, even when they weren't experiencing obvious digestive symptoms.

But here's what really gets me fired up: this connection works both ways. Just as gut inflammation can affect your brain, healing your gut can dramatically improve your mood, energy, and cognitive function. I've seen people's depression lift, brain fog clear, and energy return simply by addressing gut inflammation—without a single psychiatric medication.

When your intestines become a leaky garden hose

Let me paint you a picture of what's supposed to happen in your intestines. Imagine the lining of your gut as a highly selective security checkpoint. It's designed to let nutrients pass through into your bloodstream while keeping toxins, undigested food particles, and harmful bacteria on the other side.

This intestinal barrier is made up of tight junctions—literally tight connections between cells that act like security guards, carefully screening what gets through. When everything's working properly, it's an amazingly efficient system.

But chronic inflammation changes everything. Those tight junctions start to loosen up, creating gaps where they shouldn't be. Suddenly, things that should stay in your intestines—partially digested food proteins, bacterial toxins, inflammatory compounds—start leaking through into your bloodstream.

This is what we call "intestinal permeability" or, more commonly, "leaky gut syndrome." And despite what some conventional doctors might tell you, it's a real, measurable condition with serious health consequences.

Research from the University of Maryland shows that increased intestinal permeability is present in multiple chronic diseases, including Crohn's disease, celiac disease, multiple sclerosis, and type 1 diabetes. A study published in Clinical Gastroenterology and Hepatology found that even people without diagnosed digestive disorders often have measurable intestinal permeability that correlates with systemic inflammation.

Here's what happens when your gut becomes leaky:

Your immune system, which is heavily concentrated in your digestive tract, suddenly encounters substances that shouldn't be in your bloodstream. It does what immune systems do—it attacks. But because these foreign substances are now circulating throughout your body, the inflammatory response becomes systemic.

Your liver, which has to process all this inflammatory debris, becomes overloaded. Your immune system becomes hypervigilant, potentially developing reactions to foods you've eaten without problem for years. And the chronic inflammatory response can trigger autoimmune reactions where your immune system starts attacking your own tissues.

The research is staggering. A study from Harvard Medical School found that people with leaky gut had 3.5 times higher rates of autoimmune conditions. Research published in the World Journal of Gastroenterology showed that intestinal permeability was present in 87% of people with inflammatory joint conditions, even when they had no obvious digestive symptoms.

But here's the hopeful part: unlike some health conditions that feel permanent and unchangeable, leaky gut is remarkably responsive to dietary intervention. The cells lining your intestines regenerate every 3-5 days, which means you can literally rebuild your gut barrier faster than you might think possible.

The trillion tiny helpers living inside you

This is where the story gets really fascinating. Your digestive system isn't just yours—it's shared real estate. You're housing an entire ecosystem of microorganisms that outnumber your human cells by about 10 to 1. That's right—you're more microbe than human, at least numerically.

This microbiome, as scientists call it, isn't just along for the ride. These microscopic residents are actively involved in digestion, immune function, neurotransmitter production, inflammation regulation, and even gene expression. They're like microscopic employees working 24/7 to keep you healthy.

But here's the thing about ecosystems—they can be balanced and thriving, or they can be disrupted and dysfunctional. When your gut microbiome is balanced, the beneficial bacteria keep harmful organisms in check, support your immune system, and produce compounds that actively reduce inflammation throughout your body.

When it's disrupted—what scientists call "dysbiosis"—harmful bacteria and fungi can overgrow, producing inflammatory toxins that damage your intestinal lining and trigger systemic inflammation.

The research on microbiome and inflammation is mind-blowing:

Stanford University found that people with more diverse gut bacteria had significantly lower inflammatory markers and better immune function. The American Gut Project, which analyzed stool samples from over 15,000 people, showed that microbiome diversity was a better predictor of overall health than age, weight, or gender.

Research published in Nature showed that certain beneficial bacteria produce short-chain fatty acids that directly reduce inflammation and strengthen the intestinal barrier. These same bacteria help regulate the immune system, preventing both underactive immunity (frequent infections) and overactive immunity (autoimmune reactions).

A groundbreaking study from the University of Chicago found that the gut microbiome influences the production of over 200 different metabolites that affect everything from mood to metabolism to inflammation levels.

But here's what really amazes me: your microbiome can change dramatically within days of changing your diet. Research from Harvard shows that switching from a Western diet to a plant-rich, anti-inflammatory diet can alter gut bacteria composition within 24-48 hours.

I think about Tom, a 38-year-old who came to me with severe seasonal allergies, frequent sinus infections, and joint pain. His microbiome analysis showed very low bacterial diversity and overgrowth of inflammatory bacteria. Within eight weeks of following an anti-inflammatory diet rich in prebiotic foods, his follow-up test showed dramatic improvements in bacterial diversity. His allergies became manageable, he stopped getting frequent infections, and his joint pain decreased by about 75%.

Healing from the inside out

Once you understand that gut health affects everything from your mood to your immune function to your inflammatory status, healing becomes a whole-body project. You're not just trying to improve digestion— you're rebuilding the foundation of your health.

The beautiful thing about gut healing is that your body wants to heal. Given the right conditions, your intestinal lining can repair itself, your microbiome can rebalance, and your inflammatory status can improve dramatically.

The pillars of gut healing:

- Remove the irritants. This means identifying and eliminating foods that trigger inflammation in your specific digestive system. Common culprits include highly processed foods, artificial additives, excessive sugar, industrial seed oils, and individual trigger foods that vary from person to person.

- Replace what's missing. Many people with gut inflammation have low stomach acid, insufficient digestive enzymes, or inadequate bile production. Supporting these digestive functions can dramatically improve nutrient absorption and reduce inflammation.

- Reinoculate with beneficial bacteria. This involves both consuming probiotic-rich foods and taking targeted probiotic supplements when appropriate. But it's not just about adding bacteria—it's about creating an environment where beneficial bacteria can thrive.

- Repair the intestinal lining. Certain nutrients specifically support intestinal barrier function, including L-glutamine, zinc, omega-3 fatty acids, and compounds found in bone broth and fermented vegetables.

- Rebalance your lifestyle. Chronic stress, inadequate sleep, and lack of physical activity all negatively impact gut health. Healing requires addressing these factors alongside dietary changes.

Research from the Cleveland Clinic shows that this comprehensive approach can improve intestinal permeability by 60-80% within 12 weeks. A study published in Nutrients found that people following gut-healing protocols had significant reductions in systemic inflammatory markers, even when they weren't specifically targeting inflammation.

But what really motivates me are the transformations I've witnessed. Like Jennifer, who'd been struggling with depression and anxiety for years before discovering that her gut inflammation was affecting her neurotransmitter production. Six months of gut healing work, and she was able to discontinue her antidepressant under medical supervision.

Or Mark, whose rheumatoid arthritis symptoms improved dramatically once he addressed his underlying gut inflammation. His rheumatologist was amazed by his inflammatory marker improvements and was able to reduce his medication dosage.

The elimination diet that revealed my trigger foods

I'll be honest—when my functional medicine doctor first suggested an elimination diet, I thought it sounded like torture. Giving up multiple food groups for weeks? Tracking every symptom? It felt overwhelming and restrictive.

I was also skeptical. How could foods I'd been eating my whole life suddenly be causing problems? But my symptoms were severe enough that I was willing to try anything, so I reluctantly agreed to a structured elimination protocol.

Here's what I wish someone had told me upfront: an elimination diet isn't about permanent restriction—it's about gathering information. It's like being a detective in your own health story, systematically investigating which foods support your body and which ones work against it.

My elimination protocol involved removing the most common inflammatory foods for 4 weeks:

- Gluten-containing grains
- Dairy products
- Refined sugar and artificial sweeteners
- Industrial seed oils (soybean, corn, canola, etc.)
- Processed foods and additives
- Alcohol
- Common allergenic foods (eggs, nuts, nightshades)

The first week was rough, I won't lie. I felt deprived and couldn't figure out what to eat. But by week two, something interesting started happening. My afternoon energy crashes disappeared. My morning joint stiffness decreased noticeably. My sleep improved.

By week four, I felt better than I had in years. My brain fog lifted, my digestive issues resolved, and I had sustained energy throughout the day. It was like someone had turned up the brightness on my life.

But the real revelation came during the reintroduction phase. I systematically reintroduced each eliminated food group, one at a time, while carefully tracking my symptoms. Some foods—like gluten-free grains and most nuts—came back without any problems. Others caused immediate and obvious reactions.

Dairy was my biggest trigger. Within hours of reintroducing it, I experienced brain fog, joint stiffness, and digestive discomfort. Gluten caused similar but milder reactions. Refined sugar made me feel jittery and caused afternoon crashes.

Research from the American Journal of Gastroenterology shows that elimination diets can identify food triggers in 85% of people with chronic inflammatory symptoms. A study published in Clinical and Experimental

Allergy found that systematic food elimination and reintroduction was more accurate than blood testing for identifying problematic foods.

What I learned from my elimination experience:

First, food reactions aren't always immediate or obvious. Some of my trigger foods caused symptoms 12-24 hours after eating them, which is why I'd never made the connection before.

Second, the dose matters. Small amounts of certain trigger foods might not cause obvious symptoms, but regular consumption creates chronic low-level inflammation that accumulates over time.

Third, individual variation is huge. Foods that were problematic for me might be perfectly fine for you, and vice versa. This is why generic elimination diets don't work as well as personalized approaches.

Most importantly, I learned that I had way more control over how I felt than I'd ever realized. By avoiding my specific trigger foods and emphasizing anti-inflammatory options, I could predictably influence my energy levels, joint comfort, and overall well-being.

Testing options that actually help (and which ones to skip)

Once you understand the gut-inflammation connection, you might be tempted to jump straight into testing to figure out what's going on. While some tests can provide valuable information, others are expensive and not particularly helpful. Let me break down what's worth considering and what you can probably skip.

Tests that can provide valuable information:

- Comprehensive Stool Analysis - This can reveal information about your microbiome diversity, beneficial bacteria levels, harmful organism overgrowth, and markers of intestinal inflammation. Companies like Genova Diagnostics and Doctor's Data offer comprehensive panels that include bacterial analysis, yeast overgrowth markers, and inflammatory indicators.

  Research from the American Journal of Gastroenterology shows that comprehensive stool testing can identify treatable imbalances in 78% of people with chronic digestive and inflammatory symptoms.

- Intestinal Permeability Testing - This directly measures how "leaky" your gut lining is. The lactulose/mannitol test is the gold standard, though some newer tests use different markers. This can be particularly helpful if you have symptoms suggestive of leaky gut but want objective confirmation.

- Inflammatory Markers - Tests like high-sensitivity C-reactive protein (hs-CRP), interleukin-6, and tumor necrosis factor-alpha can provide baseline measurements of systemic inflammation and help track improvement over time.

- SIBO Testing - Small Intestinal Bacterial Overgrowth breath testing can identify bacterial overgrowth in the small intestine, which can cause symptoms similar to IBS and contribute to systemic inflammation.

Tests that are often not worth the money:

- IgG Food Sensitivity Testing - While these tests are heavily marketed, research shows they're not reliable for identifying inflammatory food triggers. A study published in the Journal of Allergy and Clinical Immunology found that IgG food panels had poor correlation with actual food reactions.

- Hair Analysis for Nutritional Status - These tests are not scientifically validated and can be misleading. Stick to blood tests for nutritional assessment.

- Generic "Leaky Gut" Panels - Many direct-consumer testing companies offer panels that claim to assess gut health but provide limited actionable information. If you're going to test, invest in comprehensive analysis from reputable labs.

- My honest take on testing: While some tests can provide helpful information, they're not necessary to start healing your gut. The elimination diet I described earlier is often more informative than expensive testing, and it costs virtually nothing.

That said, testing can be particularly valuable if you have severe symptoms, haven't responded to dietary changes, or want objective markers to track your progress. The key is working with a practitioner who can interpret results in the context of your overall health picture.

Rebuilding your inner ecosystem

Once you understand what's going on in your gut, the question becomes: how do you rebuild a healthy microbiome and heal intestinal inflammation? The good news is that your gut is remarkably resilient and responsive to positive changes.

The foundation of gut rebuilding is anti-inflammatory nutrition:

This means emphasizing foods that support beneficial bacteria growth while avoiding foods that feed harmful organisms or damage the intestinal lining. Think of it as landscaping your internal garden—you want to create conditions where the good plants thrive and the weeds can't take over.

Foods that actively heal and rebuild:

- Prebiotic-rich foods feed beneficial bacteria. These include garlic, onions, leeks, asparagus, artichokes, green bananas, and cooked-then-cooled potatoes. Research shows that prebiotic foods can increase beneficial bacteria populations within days.

- Probiotic foods introduce beneficial bacteria directly. Fermented vegetables like sauerkraut and kimchi, kefir, yogurt with live cultures, miso, and kombucha all provide beneficial organisms. The key is variety—different fermented foods contain different bacterial strains.

- Anti-inflammatory compounds found in foods like turmeric, ginger, green tea, berries, and leafy greens directly reduce intestinal inflammation and support barrier function.

- Healing nutrients like L-glutamine (found in bone broth), zinc (in pumpkin seeds and grass-fed meat), and omega-3 fatty acids (in fatty fish) specifically support intestinal lining repair.

The timeline of gut healing:

- Week 1-2: Initial inflammation reduction begins. You might notice improved digestion and less bloating.

- Week 3-4: Beneficial bacteria populations start to shift. Energy and mood improvements often become noticeable.

- Week 6-8: Intestinal barrier function begins to improve. Symptoms related to food sensitivities may decrease.

- Week 12-16: Microbiome diversity increases significantly. Systemic inflammatory markers often show improvement.

Research from Stanford University shows that gut microbiome changes can be detected within 24-48 hours of dietary changes, but significant healing of intestinal permeability typically takes 8-16 weeks.

The lifestyle factors that support gut healing:

- Stress management is crucial because chronic stress directly damages the intestinal lining and disrupts bacterial balance. Research shows that meditation, yoga, and other stress-reduction techniques can improve gut barrier function within weeks.

- Sleep quality affects gut health significantly. Poor sleep disrupts the microbiome and increases intestinal permeability. Aim for 7-9 hours of quality sleep nightly.

- Movement supports gut health by improving bacterial diversity and reducing inflammation. Even gentle walking after meals can improve digestion and bacterial balance.

- Avoiding unnecessary antibiotics helps preserve beneficial bacteria. When antibiotics are necessary, follow up with probiotic support to help restore bacterial balance.

I think about Lisa, who came to me with chronic fatigue, brain fog, and digestive issues that had been dismissed by multiple doctors as "just stress." Her comprehensive stool analysis showed very low bacterial diversity and markers of intestinal inflammation.

We started with a gentle elimination diet to identify her trigger foods (gluten and dairy were big ones), then focused on rebuilding her microbiome with prebiotic and probiotic foods. We added specific nutrients to support intestinal healing and addressed her chronic stress through meditation and yoga.

Six months later, her follow-up testing showed dramatically improved bacterial diversity and resolved inflammatory markers. More importantly, she felt like herself again—energetic, mentally clear, and free from the digestive issues that had plagued her for years.

The key to successful gut rebuilding is patience and consistency. Your microbiome didn't become imbalanced overnight, and it won't rebalance overnight either. But with consistent anti-inflammatory nutrition and lifestyle practices, most people see significant improvements within 2-3 months.

Your gut truly is your second brain, and healing it can transform not just your digestion, but your energy, mood, immune function, and overall quality of life. The trillions of microscopic helpers living inside you are waiting to support your health—you just need to give them the right environment to do their job.

CHAPTER SEVEN: It's Not Just What You Eat— The Life Factors That Fan the Flames

I used to think that if I just ate perfectly, I could overcome any other lifestyle factor that might be working against me. Perfect anti-inflammatory diet? Check. But I was still waking up exhausted, dealing with afternoon energy crashes, and feeling like my body was stuck in fight-or-flight mode most of the time.

Then I had a wake-up call that changed everything: I realized I was trying to out-eat my lifestyle.

You can consume all the turmeric and wild salmon in the world, but if you're chronically stressed, sleeping poorly, and living in a toxic environment, you're essentially trying to fill a bucket with holes in it. The inflammatory load from these lifestyle factors can overwhelm even the most perfect anti-inflammatory diet.

Here's what the research shows: lifestyle factors can influence inflammatory markers just as powerfully as diet—sometimes more so. A study published in the Journal of Health Psychology found that people with high stress levels had inflammatory marker levels similar to people eating highly inflammatory diets, even when their nutrition was otherwise excellent.

The good news? Once you understand which lifestyle factors are fanning your inflammatory flames, you can address them systematically. And unlike changing your entire diet overnight, many of these adjustments are surprisingly simple to implement.

The stress that's literally making you sick

Let me paint you a picture of my life two years ago: I'd wake up already thinking about my to-do list. I'd check my phone before my feet hit the floor. I'd rush through breakfast while mentally rehearsing the day's challenges. By 10 AM, my shoulders were already tense, and by evening, I was exhausted but wired, scrolling through social media to "relax."

Sound familiar?

Here's what I didn't understand then: chronic stress is one of the most powerful inflammatory triggers in existence. When you're stressed, your body releases cortisol and other stress hormones that directly activate inflammatory pathways. It's like having a fire alarm that never turns off—eventually, the constant noise becomes the problem itself.

The stress-inflammation cycle that's making you sick:

Research from Carnegie Mellon University shows that chronic stress can increase inflammatory markers by 200-300%. But here's the kicker: it's not just major life stressors like divorce or job loss. Daily micro-stressors—traffic, emails, news, social media, even the feeling of being perpetually behind—create the same inflammatory response when they're constant.

A groundbreaking study published in Proceedings of the National Academy of Sciences found that people with chronic stress had gene expression patterns identical to those seen in people with inflammatory diseases. The stress was literally changing how their genes functioned at the cellular level.

The Cleveland Clinic published research showing that stress-induced inflammation affects:
- Immune system function (making you more susceptible to infections)
- Digestive health (stress literally changes gut bacteria composition)
- Sleep quality (inflammatory cytokines interfere with sleep cycles)
- Brain function (neuroinflammation affects memory and mood)
- Cardiovascular health (chronic stress inflammation increases heart disease risk by 40%)

But here's what really opened my eyes: stress management techniques can reduce inflammatory markers as effectively as medication.

A study from UCLA found that people who practiced mindfulness meditation for eight weeks had 23% reductions in inflammatory markers, comparable to the effects of anti-inflammatory drugs. Research from Harvard Medical School showed that regular stress management practices could reduce C-reactive protein levels by up to 35%.

The stress management strategies that actually work:

I'm not going to tell you to "just relax more"—that's not helpful advice. What I'm going to share are specific, research-backed techniques that measurably reduce inflammatory markers:

- Box breathing: Four counts in, hold for four, out for four, hold for four. Do this for just two minutes when you feel stress rising. Research shows this activates the parasympathetic nervous system and reduces cortisol within minutes.

- The 5-4-3-2-1 grounding technique: Name 5 things you can see, 4 you can touch, 3 you can hear, 2 you can smell, 1 you can taste. This interrupts the stress response and brings you back to the present moment.

- Progressive muscle relaxation: Tense and release each muscle group for 5 seconds, starting with your toes and working up. This physically breaks the stress-tension cycle that keeps inflammatory hormones elevated.

The key isn't perfection—it's consistency. Even five minutes of stress management daily can have measurable anti-inflammatory effects.

Why your morning routine might be more important than your workout

I used to roll out of bed and immediately dive into the chaos of the day. Phone check, email scan, news scroll, and rush to get ready, grab whatever breakfast was convenient, and race out the door already feeling behind.

Then I learned something that changed everything: the first hour of your day sets your nervous system's tone for the entire day. Start in stress mode, and you'll likely stay there. Start in calm, intentional mode, and you give your body a fighting chance against inflammatory triggers.

The morning cortisol connection:

Your cortisol naturally peaks in the morning—that's normal and healthy. It's what helps you wake up and feel alert. But if you immediately flood your system with additional stressors (news, emails, rushing, inflammatory foods), you create a cortisol spike that can keep you in fight-or-flight mode all day.

Research from the University of California San Francisco found that people with chaotic morning routines had elevated inflammatory markers throughout the day, while those with calm, structured mornings had inflammation levels that naturally decreased as the day progressed.

My anti-inflammatory morning routine (and why it works):

- First 30 minutes = phone-free zone. Research shows that checking your phone immediately upon waking increases cortisol by 23% and keeps it elevated for hours. Instead, I do some light stretching, deep breathing, or just sit quietly with my coffee.

- Hydration before caffeine. I drink 16-20 ounces of water (often with a pinch of sea salt and lemon) before my first cup of coffee. Dehydration is a stress on the body that triggers inflammatory responses.

- Anti-inflammatory breakfast within 2 hours of waking. This stabilizes blood sugar and prevents the inflammatory spike that comes from either skipping breakfast or eating inflammatory foods. My go-to: chia pudding with berries and nuts, or vegetable scramble with avocado.

- 5 minutes of intentional movement. Not a workout—just gentle stretching, walking outside, or basic yoga poses. This activates circulation and helps process stress hormones.

- Gratitude or intention setting. Sounds cheesy, but research from UC Davis shows that gratitude practices reduce inflammatory markers by 16% when done consistently.

The beauty of a structured morning routine isn't that it's rigid—it's that it creates a buffer zone between sleep and the day's stresses. You're giving your nervous system time to come online gradually instead of shocking it into high alert mode.

Environmental toxins lurking in your everyday life

This was the piece of the puzzle I never saw coming. I thought I was doing everything right with my diet and stress management, but my inflammatory markers were still higher than they should have been. Then I learned about the toxic load we're all carrying from our everyday environment.

The average person is exposed to over 700 synthetic chemicals daily through food, air, water, and household products. Many of these chemicals are endocrine disruptors that trigger inflammatory responses in the body.

The hidden inflammatory triggers in your home:

- Cleaning products: Many contain volatile organic compounds (VOCs) that trigger respiratory inflammation and systemic inflammatory responses. Research from the University of Bergen found that using conventional cleaning products regularly had lung function impacts equivalent to smoking 20 cigarettes daily.

- Personal care products: The average woman uses 12 personal care products daily, exposing herself to 168 chemical ingredients. Many of these—like parabens, phthalates, and synthetic fragrances—are inflammatory triggers and endocrine disruptors.

- Plastic containers: BPA and BPS leach from plastic containers, especially when heated, and directly trigger inflammatory pathways. Research shows that people with higher BPA levels have significantly elevated inflammatory markers.

- Air quality: Indoor air is often 2-5 times more polluted than outdoor air. Poor air quality triggers respiratory inflammation that can become systemic inflammation.

- Non-stick cookware: When heated above 400°F, non-stick coatings release toxic fumes that trigger inflammatory responses and have been linked to autoimmune conditions.

Simple swaps that reduce toxic load:

- Switch to glass or stainless steel food storage containers
- Use natural cleaning products (vinegar, baking soda, castile soap work for 90% of cleaning tasks)
- Choose personal care products with fewer, more natural ingredients
- Invest in an air purifier for your bedroom and main living spaces
- Replace non-stick cookware with cast iron, stainless steel, or ceramic options
- Filter your drinking water (even basic carbon filters remove many inflammatory chemicals)

The goal isn't to live in a bubble—it's to reduce your total toxic load so your body can focus on healing instead of constantly detoxifying.

Sleep strategies that reduce inflammation while you rest

Here's something that blew my mind: sleep isn't just rest time for your body—it's active inflammation repair time. During deep sleep, your body produces anti-inflammatory compounds, clears inflammatory waste products from your brain, and repairs tissue damage caused by daily inflammatory stress.

But here's the problem: most of us aren't getting the kind of sleep that supports this healing process.

The sleep-inflammation connection:

Research from UCLA shows that just one night of poor sleep can increase inflammatory markers by 25%. Chronic sleep deprivation (less than 7 hours nightly) increases inflammatory cytokines by 40-60%, equivalent to the inflammatory load of a highly processed diet.

But it's not just quantity—it's quality. You need adequate deep sleep and REM sleep for optimal inflammatory recovery. People who get fragmented sleep (waking frequently) have higher inflammatory markers than those who sleep fewer hours but sleep deeply.

Sleep strategies that actively reduce inflammation:

- Temperature optimization: Your bedroom should be between 65-68°F. Research shows that cooler temperatures promote deeper sleep and enhance the body's natural anti-inflammatory processes.

- Complete darkness: Even small amounts of light can disrupt melatonin production. Melatonin isn't just a sleep hormone—it's also a powerful antioxidant that reduces inflammation. Blackout curtains or an eye mask are game-changers.

- The 3-2-1 rule: No food 3 hours before bed, no liquids 2 hours before bed, no screens 1 hour before bed. This prevents sleep disruption from digestion, bathroom trips, and blue light exposure.

- Magnesium before bed: 200-400mg of magnesium glycinate 1-2 hours before bed. Magnesium deficiency is incredibly common and directly contributes to both sleep problems and inflammation.

- Morning light exposure: Get 10-15 minutes of bright light (preferably sunlight) within an hour of waking. This regulates your circadian rhythm and improves sleep quality that night.

- The bedroom sanctuary approach: Your bedroom should be for sleep only. No work, no screens, no clutter. This trains your brain to associate the space with rest and recovery.

I track my sleep with a simple wearable device, and the correlation between good sleep and how I feel the next day is undeniable. Good sleep = stable energy, better mood, less joint stiffness. Poor sleep = afternoon crash, irritability, achiness.

Movement that heals instead of hurts

I used to think more exercise was always better. If a 30-minute workout was good, then 60 minutes was better, and 90 minutes was best. I was that person doing intense workouts six days a week, wondering why I felt exhausted and achy all the time.

Then I learned about the exercise-inflammation curve, and everything clicked.

The exercise paradox:

Moderate exercise is powerfully anti-inflammatory. It reduces inflammatory markers, improves immune function, and helps your body process stress hormones. But excessive exercise—especially high-intensity exercise done too frequently—becomes inflammatory itself.

Research published in the Journal of Applied Physiology shows that moderate exercise (like brisk walking for 30-45 minutes) reduces inflammatory markers by 10-15%. But excessive exercise can increase inflammatory markers by 25-50%, especially when combined with poor recovery practices.

The sweet spot for anti-inflammatory movement:

- Daily gentle movement: 20-30 minutes of walking, easy cycling, swimming, or yoga. This stimulates circulation, helps process stress hormones, and provides anti-inflammatory benefits without creating additional stress.

- Strength training 2-3 times per week: Resistance training helps build muscle mass, which is metabolically anti-inflammatory. But more than 3-4 sessions per week can become inflammatory if you're not recovering properly.

- High-intensity exercise 1-2 times per week maximum: If you love intense workouts, limit them to once or twice weekly and make sure you're getting adequate sleep, nutrition, and recovery time.

- Restorative movement daily: Gentle stretching, yoga, tai chi, or simple mobility work. This activates the parasympathetic nervous system and directly counters inflammatory stress responses.

Movement strategies that reduce inflammation:

- Post-workout nutrition timing: Eat anti-inflammatory foods within 30-60 minutes after exercise to support recovery and minimize inflammatory responses.

- Active recovery: Instead of complete rest days, do gentle movement like walking or easy yoga. This helps clear inflammatory byproducts from muscles.

- Listen to your body: If you're consistently tired, achy, or getting frequent infections, you're probably doing too much. Scale back and focus on recovery.

The goal is movement that energizes you rather than depletes you. If your exercise routine is leaving you exhausted or requiring multiple cups of coffee to get through the day, it's probably adding to your inflammatory load rather than reducing it.

Creating an anti-inflammatory home sanctuary

Your home environment should be your anti-inflammatory refuge—a place where your body can relax, recover, and heal. But many of our homes are actually adding to our inflammatory burden without us realizing it.

The anti-inflammatory home audit:

- Air quality: Invest in plants that naturally purify air (snake plants, spider plants, peace lilies). Consider an air purifier for bedrooms and main living areas. Change HVAC filters regularly and avoid synthetic air fresheners.

- Lighting: Use warm, dim lighting in the evening to support natural melatonin production. Consider salt lamps or warm LED bulbs instead of harsh fluorescent lighting.

- Clutter reduction: Physical clutter creates mental stress, which triggers inflammatory responses. A clean, organized space promotes calm and reduces cortisol levels.

- Natural materials: Choose natural fiber bedding, rugs, and furniture when possible. Synthetic materials often off-gas chemicals that can trigger inflammatory responses.

- Electronics management: Create phone-free zones and times. Keep electronics out of the bedroom. The EMF exposure from constant electronic use may contribute to inflammatory responses in sensitive individuals.

- Sound environment: Reduce noise pollution with soft furnishings, rugs, and curtains. Consider a white noise machine or earplugs if you live in a noisy area.

- Temperature control: Keep your home slightly cool (68-72°F) during the day and cooler (65-68°F) at night to support optimal sleep and reduce inflammatory stress.

The power of saying no (to inflammation-triggering situations)

This might be the most important section in this entire chapter, because it's about recognizing that some people, situations, and commitments are literally inflammatory to your health.

The relationship inflammation connection:

Research from Ohio State University found that people in chronically stressful relationships had inflammatory marker levels 40% higher than those in supportive relationships. The stress of difficult relationships creates the same inflammatory response as eating a highly inflammatory diet daily.

Inflammatory situations to recognize:

- Toxic relationships: People who consistently drain your energy, create drama, or make you feel stressed or anxious after interactions.

- Overcommitment: Saying yes to everything because you don't want to disappoint people, even when it overwhelms your schedule and stress levels.

- News and social media overload: Constant exposure to negative news and social media comparison creates chronic stress responses that trigger inflammation.

- Work environments: Jobs that create chronic stress, don't allow for breaks, or involve toxic workplace dynamics.

- Social obligations: Events or activities you attend out of guilt rather than genuine enjoyment.

The art of anti-inflammatory boundaries:

- The 24-hour rule: Don't commit to anything immediately. Give yourself 24 hours to consider whether it aligns with your health and energy levels.

- Energy audit: After social interactions, notice how you feel. Energized or drained? This tells you whether the relationship is supporting or undermining your health.

- Media boundaries: Limit news consumption to 15-30 minutes daily. Unfollow social media accounts that make you feel inadequate or anxious.

- Schedule protection: Block out time for rest, meal preparation, and self-care. Treat these appointments as seriously as you would any other commitment.

- The gentle no: "I can't commit to that right now, but thank you for thinking of me." You don't owe anyone a detailed explanation for protecting your health.

Learning to say no to inflammatory situations was one of the hardest but most important skills I developed. It's not selfish—it's necessary. You can't pour from an empty cup, and you can't heal from chronic inflammation while constantly exposing yourself to inflammatory stressors.

The beautiful thing about addressing these lifestyle factors is that they work synergistically with your anti-inflammatory diet. Better sleep improves your food choices. Less stress makes you crave inflammatory foods less. A cleaner environment supports better sleep. Movement improves stress resilience.

It's all connected, and when you start addressing these factors together, the results compound in ways that will surprise you. You're not just eating your way to better health—you're living your way there.

CHAPTER EIGHT: Your 30-Day Fresh Start—A Gentle Reset That Actually Works

Okay, let's talk about the elephant in the room. You've probably tried 30-day challenges before. Maybe you've done elimination diets, detoxes, or other "reset" programs that left you feeling deprived, obsessive, or ultimately unsuccessful. I get it—the internet is full of extreme approaches that promise miraculous results if you just follow their rigid rules perfectly.

This isn't that.

What I'm offering you is a gentle, sustainable approach to discovering how different foods affect your body's inflammatory responses. It's not about perfection or deprivation—it's about curiosity and self-discovery. Think of it as a month-long experiment where you're both the scientist and the subject, gathering data about what makes you feel amazing versus what makes you feel awful.

The research backing this approach is solid. A study published in the Journal of Nutrition found that people following structured anti-inflammatory eating plans for 30 days showed measurable improvements in inflammatory markers, energy levels, and quality of life scores. But more importantly, 78% of participants continued with the eating pattern six months later because they felt so much better.

Here's what makes this different: we're not counting calories, weighing food, or following complicated meal plans. We're simply removing the most common inflammatory triggers for 30 days while flooding your body with anti-inflammatory nutrients. Then we're paying close attention to how that makes you feel.

Week 1: Clearing the deck (what to expect and how to prepare)

The Mental Game: Setting Yourself Up for Success

Before we talk about food, let's talk about mindset. Week 1 is about preparation—both practical and psychological. This isn't a punishment or a test of willpower. It's an investment in understanding your body better.

I want you to think of yourself as a detective gathering clues, not a prisoner serving time. Every meal is data. Every day is information. You're not "being good" or "being bad"—you're being curious.

The Practical Prep: Getting Your Environment Ready

Research from Cornell University shows that environmental factors influence 90% of our food decisions. Translation: if inflammatory foods are easily accessible and anti-inflammatory foods require effort, you're fighting an uphill battle.

Here's your Week 1 prep checklist:

Kitchen Cleanup (15 minutes, maximum):
- Remove the most tempting inflammatory foods from easy reach
- You don't have to throw anything away—just put it where you won't see it constantly
- Stock your counter with anti-inflammatory snacks: nuts, seeds, and fresh fruit
- Fill your fridge with pre-washed vegetables and prepared proteins

Mental Preparation:
- Tell supportive friends and family what you're doing
- Plan for challenging situations (work lunches, social events, and stress eating triggers)
- Identify your personal motivation—what do you hope to feel different about in 30 days?

What to Expect in Week 1:

Days 1-3 might feel like withdrawal from inflammatory foods, especially if you're used to high amounts of sugar or processed foods. Research from Princeton University shows that sugar can create addiction-like responses in the brain, so some people experience mild withdrawal symptoms including:
- Cravings for sweet or salty foods
- Slight fatigue or irritability
- Headaches (usually mild and short-lived)

This is normal and temporary. It's actually a sign that your body is starting to reset its inflammatory responses.

Days 4-7 often bring the first glimpses of improvement:
- Energy levels starting to stabilize
- Better sleep quality
- Reduced bloating or digestive discomfort
- Clearer thinking

Your Week 1 Focus Foods:

Emphasize these anti-inflammatory powerhouses:
- Fatty fish (salmon, sardines, and mackerel) - aim for 2-3 servings
- Leafy greens (spinach, kale, arugula) - daily
- Colorful vegetables (bell peppers, carrots, beets) - variety is key
- Berries and low-glycemic fruits (blueberries, cherries, apples)
- Nuts and seeds (walnuts, almonds, chia seeds, flaxseeds)

- Olive oil and avocados - your primary fats
- Herbs and spices (turmeric, ginger, garlic) - use liberally

Temporarily avoid these common inflammatory triggers:
- Added sugars and artificial sweeteners
- Refined grains and processed foods
- Industrial seed oils (soybean, corn, and canola)
- Conventional dairy products
- Processed meats
- Alcohol

Week 1 Reality Check:
You don't have to be perfect. If you slip up, that's data too. Notice how you feel after eating something inflammatory, then get back on track with your next meal. Research shows that consistency over perfection is what creates lasting change.

Week 2: Finding your rhythm (when the magic starts happening)

This is where things get interesting. Week 2 is typically when people start experiencing what I call the "anti-inflammatory breakthrough"—that moment when you realize you actually feel noticeably different.

What the Research Says About Week 2:
Studies show that inflammatory markers begin to decrease measurably around day 10-14 of consistent anti-inflammatory eating. C-reactive protein levels can drop by 15-20%, and people report significant improvements in energy, sleep, and overall well-being.

Common Week 2 Experiences:

- Energy Stabilization: That afternoon crash that used to hit like a wall? It might just... not happen. Instead of reaching for caffeine or sugar at 3 PM, you might find yourself still feeling steady and focused.

- Sleep Improvements: Many people notice they're falling asleep easier and waking up more refreshed. Chronic inflammation interferes with sleep cycles, so as inflammation decreases, sleep quality often improves dramatically.

- Digestive Comfort: Bloating, gas, and digestive discomfort often decrease significantly. The gut lining begins to heal when you remove inflammatory triggers and add gut-supporting foods.

- Mental Clarity: That brain fog that made you feel like you were thinking through molasses? It often starts lifting in Week 2. Neuroinflammation decreases, and cognitive function improves.

- Physical Comfort: Joint stiffness, muscle aches, and general physical discomfort often begin to decrease. Morning stiffness might reduce from 30 minutes to 10 minutes, or disappear entirely.

Your Week 2 Strategy: Building Sustainable Habits

Week 2 is about finding your rhythm and making anti-inflammatory eating feel natural rather than forced. Research from the University College London shows that it takes an average of 66 days to form a new habit, but the foundation is built in the first few weeks.

Meal Rhythm Development:
- Start recognizing which meals make you feel energized versus sluggish
- Notice how different combinations of foods affect your satiety and energy
- Pay attention to timing—when do you feel best eating your largest meals?

Cooking Confidence:
- Master 2-3 simple anti-inflammatory meals you can make without thinking
- Experiment with new herbs and spices to keep things interesting
- Develop a prep routine that works for your lifestyle

Social Navigation:
- Practice explaining your eating approach in social situations
- Develop strategies for restaurants and social events
- Find supportive friends or family members who encourage your journey

Week 2 Common Challenges and Solutions:

* Challenge: "I'm getting bored with the food"
* Solution: This is where creativity kicks in. Try new vegetables, experiment with different cooking methods, and explore cuisines that are naturally anti-inflammatory (Mediterranean, Japanese, and Indian with the right spices).

* Challenge: "I had a bad day and ate inflammatory foods"
* Solution: Notice how you feel afterward without judgment. Did you feel more tired the next day? More achy? This is valuable data, not a failure.

* Challenge: "People are commenting on my eating"
* Solution: You don't owe anyone an explanation, but having a simple response ready helps: "I'm experimenting with foods that make me feel better."

Week 3: Fine-tuning your approach (listening to your body's whispers)

Week 3 is where you become fluent in your body's language. You've cleared out the inflammatory noise, and now you can hear the subtle signals your body has been trying to send you for years.

The Body Wisdom Awakening: Research from Harvard Medical School shows that chronic inflammation literally interferes with our ability to sense hunger, satiety, and food preferences. As inflammation decreases, our natural body wisdom—our innate ability to know what foods make us feel good—returns.

What Week 3 Typically Brings:

- Refined Sensitivity: You might notice that you can now feel the effects of foods much more clearly. A meal that supports your energy versus one that drains it becomes obvious within an hour or two.

- Natural Portion Control: Many people find they naturally eat less without trying because anti-inflammatory foods are more satisfying and their hunger/satiety signals are working properly again.

- Craving Changes: Those intense cravings for sugar or processed foods often diminish significantly. Instead, you might find yourself craving vegetables, quality proteins, or other whole foods.

- Mood Stability: Emotional ups and downs often level out as neuroinflammation decreases and blood sugar stabilizes.

Your Week 3 Fine-Tuning Process:

Individual Tolerance Testing: Not everyone reacts to foods the same way. Week 3 is when you start paying attention to your personal patterns:

- Do nightshades (tomatoes, peppers, eggplant) seem to increase your joint pain?
- Does dairy cause digestive issues or skin problems for you specifically?
- Are there certain grains that make you feel sluggish while others don't?
- Do you feel better with more protein or more healthy fats?

Energy Optimization:
- Notice which meals give you sustained energy versus quick energy followed by a crash
- Pay attention to meal timing—do you feel better eating larger meals earlier in the day?
- Observe how different foods affect your sleep quality

Digestive Fine-Tuning:
- Are there healthy foods that don't agree with you? (Even healthy foods can be problematic for some people)
- Do you feel better with cooked vegetables versus raw?
- How do different fiber sources affect your digestion?

Week 3 Advanced Strategies:

- Nutrient Timing: Some people find they feel better having their largest meal earlier in the day, while others prefer smaller, frequent meals. There's no right answer—only what works for your body.

- Preparation Methods: You might discover that you tolerate certain foods better when they're prepared differently. For example, some people digest vegetables better when they're lightly cooked rather than raw.

- Combination Effects: Pay attention to how different food combinations affect you. You might find that adding healthy fats to vegetables improves how you feel, or that certain protein and carbohydrate combinations work better for your energy levels.

Week 4: Planning for the long haul (making this your new normal)

Week 4 isn't about the finish line—it's about the starting line. You've spent three weeks gathering data about how foods affect your body. Now it's time to turn that knowledge into a sustainable lifestyle.

The Sustainability Question: Research from the American Journal of Lifestyle Medicine shows that dietary changes are only effective long-term if they become integrated into daily life rather than viewed as temporary interventions. The people who maintain anti-inflammatory eating patterns long-term are those who focus on how the foods make them feel rather than following external rules.

Your Week 4 Integration Strategy:

Identify Your Non-Negotiables:
By now, you probably have a clear sense of which foods consistently make you feel good and which ones consistently make you feel awful. Your non-negotiables are the foods that have such a clear positive or negative impact that avoiding or including them becomes automatic.

Create Your Personal Guidelines:
Instead of rigid rules, develop flexible guidelines based on your experience:
- "I feel best when I include anti-inflammatory fats with every meal"
- "I have more energy when I limit refined sugars"
- "My joints feel better when I emphasize colorful vegetables"
- "I sleep better when I don't eat late in the evening"

Plan for Real Life:
- How will you handle social situations?
- What are your go-to meals when you're stressed or busy?
- How will you maintain your approach during travel or schedule changes?
- What support systems do you need to stay consistent?

The 80/20 Principle:
Research suggests that being consistent with anti-inflammatory eating 80% of the time provides most of the health benefits while allowing for flexibility and social enjoyment. Perfect adherence isn't necessary—consistent adherence is.

CHAPTER NINE: When You Need Extra Support— Tailoring This Approach for Your Specific Situation

You know what I've learned after years of helping people navigate anti-inflammatory eating? One size definitely doesn't fit all. While the core principles remain the same—reduce inflammatory foods, increase anti-inflammatory ones—how you apply these principles can make all the difference depending on what your body is dealing with.

Think of this chapter as your personalized roadmap. Maybe you picked up this book because of joint pain that's making mornings miserable. Or perhaps you're managing diabetes and wondering how inflammation fits into your blood sugar struggles. Whatever brought you here, this chapter will help you fine-tune the anti-inflammatory approach for your specific situation.

I'm not trying to replace your doctor or specialist—I'm giving you tools to work alongside them more effectively. Consider this your guide to becoming an informed advocate for your own health.

For my friends fighting arthritis and joint pain

If you wake up every morning feeling like you're 90 years old, or if climbing stairs has become an exercise in endurance, you're not alone. Arthritis affects over 54 million Americans, and joint pain is one of the leading causes of disability worldwide. But here's what most people don't realize: the pain you're experiencing isn't just wear and tear—it's inflammation, and that means you can do something about it.

The arthritis-inflammation connection runs deep. Research from the Arthritis Foundation shows that people with osteoarthritis—the "wear and tear" kind—actually have elevated inflammatory markers throughout their bodies, not just in affected joints. This systemic inflammation can accelerate joint damage and increase pain levels.

For rheumatoid arthritis, the connection is even more direct. RA is fundamentally an inflammatory condition where your immune system attacks joint tissue. But studies show that dietary intervention can reduce RA symptoms by up to 40% in some people.

Your joint-specific anti-inflammatory strategy:

- Prioritize omega-3 powerhouses. Research published in the Annals of Rheumatic Diseases found that people consuming at least 2 grams of EPA and DHA daily (from fish or supplements) experienced 25-30%

reductions in joint pain and morning stiffness. Think wild-caught salmon, sardines, mackerel, and anchovies at least three times per week. If you're not a fish person, consider a high-quality fish oil supplement—but aim for food sources first.

- Embrace the spice cabinet. Turmeric contains curcumin, which studies show can be as effective as ibuprofen for joint pain without the side effects. The key is absorption—combine turmeric with black pepper and a healthy fat like olive oil. Research from the University of Arizona found that people taking 1,000mg of curcumin daily had significant improvements in joint function within 8 weeks.

  Ginger is another powerhouse. A study in the International Journal of Rheumatic Diseases showed that 1 teaspoon of fresh ginger daily reduced inflammatory markers and pain scores in people with osteoarthritis.

- Load up on anthocyanins. These are the compounds that make berries red, blue, and purple. Research shows they specifically target the inflammatory pathways involved in joint pain. Tart cherries are particularly potent—studies show that drinking 8 ounces of tart cherry juice daily can reduce arthritis pain by up to 25%.

- Consider the nightshade question. About 10-15% of people with arthritis find that nightshade vegetables (tomatoes, potatoes, peppers, eggplant) worsen their symptoms. The compound solanine in these foods can trigger inflammation in sensitive individuals. Try eliminating nightshades for 4 weeks and see if your pain improves.

- What to avoid like your joints depend on it: Refined carbohydrates and added sugars create inflammatory compounds called advanced glycation end products (AGEs) that can accelerate joint damage. Processed meats contain inflammatory compounds that specifically worsen arthritis symptoms. Trans fats and excessive omega-6 oils fuel inflammatory pathways.

I think about Margaret, a 58-year-old teacher who was considering early retirement because her rheumatoid arthritis made it hard to write on the board or grade papers. After six months of targeted anti-inflammatory eating, her morning stiffness decreased from 2 hours to 20 minutes, and she was able to reduce one of her medications with her rheumatologist's approval.

Special considerations for autoimmune warriors

Living with an autoimmune condition means your immune system has forgotten how to distinguish friend from foe. It's attacking your own tissues—whether that's joints in rheumatoid arthritis, the digestive tract in Crohn's disease, or skin cells in psoriasis.

The conventional medical approach focuses on suppressing immune function to reduce this attack, which can be lifesaving but often comes with significant side effects. Anti-inflammatory eating offers a complementary approach: instead of just suppressing symptoms, you're addressing some of the underlying triggers that keep your immune system in overdrive.

Research from the Journal of Autoimmunity shows that dietary intervention can reduce autoimmune disease activity by 20-50% in many cases. More importantly, people following anti-inflammatory protocols often experience better quality of life, reduced fatigue, and fewer flares.

Your autoimmune-specific protocol:

- Consider an elimination approach. Many autoimmune conditions involve food sensitivities that keep the immune system activated. The most common triggers are gluten, dairy, eggs, soy, corn, and nuts. Research shows that eliminating these foods for 30 days, then reintroducing them one at a time, can identify personal triggers in about 75% of people with autoimmune conditions.

- Heal the gut barrier. Intestinal permeability ("leaky gut") is found in most autoimmune conditions. Focus on gut-healing foods like bone broth, fermented vegetables, and prebiotic-rich foods. L-glutamine supplementation (5-10 grams daily) has shown promise in research for healing intestinal lining.

- Prioritize anti-inflammatory fats. Research from the American Journal of Clinical Nutrition shows that people with autoimmune conditions need higher amounts of omega-3 fatty acids—aim for 3-4 grams of combined EPA and DHA daily from food and supplements.

- Support detoxification. Autoimmune conditions often involve impaired detoxification pathways. Include sulfur-rich vegetables like broccoli, cauliflower, and brussels sprouts. Add cilantro and parsley to help with heavy metal elimination.

- Mind the molecular mimicry. Some food proteins can trigger immune responses because they look similar to your own tissues. This is highly individual, but common culprits include gluten (which can mimic thyroid tissue), dairy proteins (which can mimic joint tissue), and certain lectins in grains and legumes.

- Timing matters. Many people with autoimmune conditions benefit from time-restricted eating—giving their digestive system a 12-14 hour break between dinner and breakfast. This supports cellular cleanup processes and reduces systemic inflammation.

Jessica's story illustrates this beautifully. She'd been battling lupus for eight years, dealing with joint pain, fatigue, and frequent flares. Through careful elimination and reintroduction, she discovered that gluten and dairy were major triggers. Six months after eliminating these foods and focusing on gut healing, her inflammatory markers dropped by 60%, and she went from having monthly flares to having none in over a year.

Heart health and inflammation (the connection that could save your life)

Here's something that might surprise you: heart disease isn't just about cholesterol. In fact, research shows that inflammation is often a better predictor of heart attack risk than cholesterol levels. The famous JUPITER trial found that people with low cholesterol but high inflammation had higher cardiovascular risk than people with high cholesterol but low inflammation.

This changes everything about how we approach heart health. Yes, cholesterol matters, but inflammation is often the match that lights the fire.

Studies show that anti-inflammatory eating can reduce cardiovascular risk by up to 30%—that's better than most medications, with the side effects being increased energy and better overall health.

Your heart-protective anti-inflammatory strategy:

- Make the Mediterranean your model. The Mediterranean diet is essentially an anti-inflammatory eating pattern, and the research is overwhelming. The PREDIMED study showed 30% reductions in cardiovascular events. Focus on olive oil, fatty fish, nuts, seeds, vegetables, and moderate amounts of red wine if you drink alcohol.

- Embrace the nitric oxide foods. Leafy greens, beets, and pomegranates contain nitrates that your body converts to nitric oxide—a compound that relaxes blood vessels and reduces inflammation. Research shows that drinking beet juice can lower blood pressure within hours.

- Consider the fiber factor. Soluble fiber feeds beneficial gut bacteria, which produce compounds that directly reduce cardiovascular inflammation. Aim for 35-40 grams daily from oats, beans, apples, and vegetables.

- Watch the inflammatory oils. This is crucial for heart health. Excessive omega-6 oils (corn, soy, sunflower, and safflower) can increase cardiovascular inflammation. Stick to olive oil, avocado oil, and coconut oil for cooking.

- Mind your blood sugar. High blood sugar creates inflammatory compounds that damage blood vessels. Focus on low-glycemic foods and consider pairing carbs with protein or healthy fats to blunt blood sugar spikes.

- Don't forget magnesium. This mineral is crucial for heart rhythm and blood vessel function. Leafy greens, nuts, seeds, and dark chocolate are excellent sources. Research shows that people with higher magnesium intake have 30% lower risk of heart disease.

Robert's transformation exemplifies this approach. At 52, he'd already had one heart attack and was on multiple medications. His cardiologist supported his decision to adopt anti-inflammatory eating alongside his medical treatment. Eight months later, his C-reactive protein dropped from 8.2 to 1.1 (normal), his blood pressure improved enough to reduce one medication, and his energy levels were the best they'd been in years.

Managing diabetes and blood sugar spikes

If you're dealing with type 2 diabetes or prediabetes, understanding the inflammation connection could be a game-changer. Type 2 diabetes isn't just about blood sugar—it's fundamentally an inflammatory condition. Chronic inflammation interferes with insulin signaling, leading to insulin resistance and eventually diabetes.

Research from the Joslin Diabetes Center shows that reducing systemic inflammation can improve insulin sensitivity even before significant weight loss occurs. This means that anti-inflammatory eating can help with blood sugar control independent of its effects on body weight.

Your blood sugar-stabilizing anti-inflammatory approach:

- Focus on the glycemic load, not just glycemic index. It's not just about how quickly foods raise blood sugar, but how much they raise it overall. Choose foods that are both low glycemic and low in overall carbs when blood sugar control is a priority.

- Prioritize protein and fiber. These nutrients slow sugar absorption and reduce inflammatory spikes that occur after meals. Research shows that eating protein or fiber before carbohydrates can reduce post-meal blood sugar spikes by 20-30%.

- Embrace cinnamon and chromium. Cinnamon contains compounds that improve insulin sensitivity. Studies show that 1-2 teaspoons daily can reduce fasting blood sugar by 10-15%. Chromium-rich foods like broccoli and nutritional yeast also support healthy blood sugar metabolism.

- Consider apple cider vinegar. Research shows that 1-2 tablespoons before meals can reduce post-meal blood sugar spikes by up to 25%. The acetic acid appears to slow carbohydrate absorption.

- Time your carbs. If you're going to eat higher-carb foods, have them earlier in the day when insulin sensitivity is naturally higher, and pair them with physical activity when possible.

- Watch for hidden sugars. Many foods marketed as "healthy" contain inflammatory sugars. Read labels carefully and avoid anything with more than 6 grams of added sugar per serving.

- Support your liver. Your liver plays a crucial role in blood sugar regulation. Foods like milk thistle, dandelion greens, and artichokes support liver function and can improve blood sugar control.

Maria's experience illustrates this perfectly. She'd been prediabetic for three years, watching her fasting glucose creep higher despite her doctor's warnings. After adopting anti-inflammatory eating principles, her HbA1c dropped from 6.2% to 5.4% in four months, and her inflammatory markers normalized for the first time in years.

Skin conditions that heal from the inside out

Your skin is your body's largest organ and often the first place inflammation shows up visually. Whether you're dealing with acne, eczema, psoriasis, or just dull, lifeless skin, the solution often lies in addressing systemic inflammation rather than just treating the surface.

Research published in the Journal of Investigative Dermatology found that people with inflammatory skin conditions have elevated systemic inflammatory markers, not just local skin inflammation. This means that what's happening on your skin reflects what's happening throughout your body.

Your skin-healing anti-inflammatory protocol:

- Address the gut-skin axis. Research shows a strong connection between gut health and skin conditions. About 70% of people with skin issues have some degree of digestive dysfunction. Focus on fermented foods, prebiotic fibers, and gut-healing nutrients like zinc and L-glutamine.

- Eliminate dairy temporarily. Multiple studies link dairy consumption to acne and eczema. The hormones and inflammatory proteins in dairy can trigger skin inflammation in sensitive individuals. Try eliminating all dairy for 6 weeks and see if your skin improves.

- Load up on skin-supporting nutrients. Vitamin A (from sweet potatoes, carrots, leafy greens) supports skin cell turnover. Vitamin C (from berries, citrus, bell peppers) is crucial for collagen production. Zinc (from pumpkin seeds, oysters, and grass-fed beef) has anti-inflammatory effects on skin.

- Consider the histamine connection. Some people with skin conditions have histamine intolerance, which can trigger inflammation and skin reactions. Common high-histamine foods include aged cheeses, fermented foods, wine, and processed meats.

- Support detoxification. Your skin is one of your detox organs. When your liver and kidneys are overwhelmed, toxins can be eliminated through skin, causing inflammation. Support detox with cruciferous vegetables, plenty of water, and liver-supporting herbs like milk thistle.

- Mind your omega ratios. The typical Western diet has too much omega-6 (inflammatory) and too little omega-3 (anti-inflammatory). This imbalance directly affects skin inflammation. Aim for a 4:1 or better omega-6 to omega-3 ratio.

Lisa's transformation was remarkable. She'd struggled with cystic acne for 15 years, trying every topical treatment and antibiotic without lasting success. After eliminating dairy and refined sugars while focusing on gut health and anti-inflammatory foods, her skin cleared dramatically within 12 weeks. Two years later, she rarely has breakouts and credits the dietary changes with finally giving her confidence back.

Digestive issues that finally make sense

If you're dealing with IBS, IBD, GERD, or other digestive issues, you already know that what you eat affects how you feel. But you might not realize that digestive inflammation can trigger systemic inflammation throughout your body, and vice versa.

The gut is home to 70% of your immune system and produces many of the same inflammatory compounds found elsewhere in your body. When your digestive tract is inflamed, it sends inflammatory signals throughout your system. When you have systemic inflammation, it can worsen digestive symptoms.

Your gut-healing anti-inflammatory approach:

- Identify and eliminate trigger foods. The most common inflammatory triggers for digestive issues are gluten, dairy, soy, corn, eggs, and nuts. But this is highly individual—your triggers might be completely different. An elimination diet followed by systematic reintroduction is the gold standard for identifying personal triggers.

- Heal the intestinal lining. Focus on gut-healing nutrients like L-glutamine (5-15 grams daily), zinc (15-30mg daily), and omega-3 fatty acids. Bone broth provides collagen and glycine, which support intestinal repair.

- Support beneficial bacteria. Include fermented foods like sauerkraut, kimchi, and kefir (if you tolerate dairy). Prebiotic foods like garlic, onions, Jerusalem artichokes, and green bananas feed beneficial bacteria.

- Consider digestive support. Many people with digestive issues have low stomach acid or insufficient digestive enzymes. Bitter foods like arugula and dandelion greens stimulate digestive juices. Some people benefit from betaine HCl or digestive enzyme supplements.

- Mind the FODMAP connection. Some people with IBS are sensitive to fermentable carbohydrates called FODMAPs. These are found in certain fruits, vegetables, grains, and legumes. A low-FODMAP elimination diet can identify if these are problematic for you.

- Manage stress. The gut-brain connection is real and powerful. Chronic stress directly increases intestinal inflammation and permeability. Stress management techniques aren't optional for gut healing—they're essential.

David's journey with Crohn's disease illustrates the power of this approach. After multiple surgeries and years of medication with limited success, he was facing another surgery when he decided to try dietary intervention. Through careful elimination and gut healing protocols, he achieved remission and has been surgery-free for over three years.

Brain fog, memory, and cognitive health

If you've ever felt like your brain is wrapped in cotton, if you forget words mid-sentence, or if you just can't think as clearly as you used to, you're experiencing neuroinflammation. This is inflammation specifically affecting brain tissue, and it's more common than you might think.

Research shows that systemic inflammation can cross the blood-brain barrier and trigger inflammatory responses in brain tissue. This neuroinflammation interferes with neurotransmitter production, disrupts sleep patterns, and affects memory consolidation.

Studies from Harvard Medical School found that people with higher inflammatory markers had faster rates of cognitive decline and smaller brain volumes over time. The good news? Research also shows that anti-inflammatory interventions can slow and sometimes reverse these changes.

Your brain-protective anti-inflammatory strategy:

- Prioritize omega-3 DHA. Your brain is about 60% fat, and DHA makes up a significant portion of brain tissue. Research shows that people with higher DHA levels have larger brain volumes and better cognitive function. Aim for 1-2 grams of DHA daily from fatty fish or algae-based supplements.

- Embrace brain berries. Blueberries, blackberries, and other dark berries contain compounds that specifically protect brain cells from inflammation. The Nurses' Health Study found that women eating the most berries had cognitive function equivalent to being 2.5 years younger.

- Consider the ketone connection. Your brain can use ketones as an alternative fuel source, and ketones have anti-inflammatory effects on brain tissue. You don't need to follow a ketogenic diet, but including MCT oil or coconut oil can provide brain-protective ketones.

- Support the blood-brain barrier. This protective barrier prevents inflammatory compounds from entering your brain, but chronic inflammation can make it "leaky." Foods rich in flavonoids (dark chocolate, green tea, berries) help maintain blood-brain barrier integrity.

- Mind your B vitamins. Deficiencies in B6, B12, and folate can increase brain inflammation and cognitive decline. Include leafy greens, eggs, fish, and consider a high-quality B-complex supplement.

- Consider curcumin. This compound from turmeric can cross the blood-brain barrier and has specific anti-inflammatory effects on brain tissue. Studies show it may help clear amyloid plaques associated with Alzheimer's disease.

- Don't forget magnesium. This mineral is crucial for neurotransmitter function and has calming effects on the nervous system. Many people are deficient, and deficiency can worsen brain fog and anxiety.

Patricia's story demonstrates this beautifully. At 55, she was terrified by increasing forgetfulness and brain fog that was affecting her work performance. Her doctor said it was "normal aging," but she knew something was wrong. After adopting brain-protective anti-inflammatory eating, her mental clarity returned within 6 weeks. A year later, she feels sharper than she has in a decade.

Remember, these aren't quick fixes or miracle cures. They're evidence-based strategies for addressing the inflammatory processes underlying many chronic health issues. Work with your healthcare providers, track your symptoms, and give your body time to heal.

The beautiful thing about anti-inflammatory eating is that even if you're focusing on one specific condition, you're likely to see improvements in other areas too. When you calm systemic inflammation, your whole body benefits. Your energy improves, your sleep gets better, your mood stabilizes, and you start to feel like yourself again.

That's the power of addressing root causes instead of just managing symptoms. Your body wants to heal— sometimes it just needs the right support to remember how.

BREAKFAST & FIRST MEALS

Golden Turmeric Chia Pudding

Prep Time: 5 minutes Chill Time: 4 hours or overnight Serves: 2

1/4 cup chia seeds
1 cup unsweetened coconut milk
1 tsp ground turmeric
1/2 tsp ground ginger
1/4 tsp ground cinnamon

1 tbsp raw honey or maple syrup
1/4 cup fresh blueberries
2 tbsp chopped walnuts
Pinch of black pepper

1. Whisk together chia seeds, coconut milk, turmeric, ginger, cinnamon, honey, and black pepper in a bowl.
2. Let sit for 5 minutes, then whisk again to prevent clumping.
3. Cover and refrigerate for at least 4 hours or overnight.
4. Serve topped with blueberries and walnuts.

Wild Salmon and Avocado Scramble

Prep Time: 5 minutes Cook Time: 8 minutes Serves: 2

4 omega-3 enriched eggs
4 oz wild-caught smoked salmon, flaked
1 ripe avocado, sliced
2 tbsp extra virgin olive oil
2 tbsp fresh dill, chopped
1 tbsp fresh chives, chopped

1/4 red onion, thinly sliced
Fresh spinach leaves
Sea salt and black pepper to taste

1. Heat olive oil in a non-stick pan over medium-low heat.
2. Whisk eggs and scramble gently until just set.
3. Add flaked salmon and fresh herbs in the last minute.
4. Serve over spinach with avocado slices and red onion.
5. Season with salt and pepper.

Green Smoothie Bowl

Prep Time: 8 minutes Serves: 1

1 cup fresh spinach
1/2 frozen banana
1/2 cup frozen pineapple chunks
1/2 avocado
1 tbsp ground flaxseed

1 cup unsweetened almond milk
1 tsp fresh ginger, grated
1 tbsp almond butter
Toppings: coconut flakes, hemp seeds, fresh berries

1. Blend all ingredients except toppings until smooth and creamy.
2. Pour into a bowl and add desired toppings.
3. Serve.

Sweet Potato and Kale Hash with Poached Eggs

Prep Time: 10 minutes Cook Time: 20 minutes Serves: 2

2 medium sweet potatoes, diced small
2 cups fresh kale, chopped
4 eggs
3 tbsp avocado oil
1/2 red bell pepper, diced
1/4 red onion, diced
2 cloves garlic, minced

1 tsp smoked paprika
1/2 tsp ground cumin
Sea salt and pepper to taste

1. Heat avocado oil in a large skillet over medium heat.
2. Add sweet potatoes and cook for 12-15 minutes until tender.
3. Add onion, bell pepper, and garlic; cook 3 minutes.
4. Add kale and spices; cook until kale wilts.
5. Poach eggs and serve over hash.

Coconut Berry Quinoa Breakfast Bowl

Prep Time: 5 minutes Cook Time: 15 minutes Serves: 2

1 cup cooked quinoa
1 can (400ml) coconut milk
1/2 cup mixed berries (blueberries, raspberries)
2 tbsp unsweetened coconut flakes
1 tbsp chia seeds
1 tbsp raw honey

1/2 tsp vanilla extract
1/4 tsp ground cinnamon
Sliced almonds for topping

. Heat coconut milk in a saucepan over medium heat.
2. Add cooked quinoa, cinnamon, and vanilla.
3. Simmer for 5 minutes until creamy.
4. Add honey and half the berries.
5. Serve topped with remaining berries, coconut flakes, chia seeds, and almonds.

Mediterranean Vegetable Frittata

Prep Time: 15 minutes Cook Time: 25 minutes Serves: 4

8 eggs
1 zucchini, sliced
1 red bell pepper, sliced
1/2 cup sun-dried tomatoes, chopped
1/4 cup kalamata olives, pitted and halved
2 tbsp extra virgin olive oil

2 tbsp fresh basil, chopped
1 tbsp fresh oregano
1/4 cup fresh parsley
Sea salt and pepper to taste

1. Preheat oven to 375°F (190°C).
2. Heat olive oil in an oven-safe skillet over medium heat.
3. Sauté zucchini and bell pepper for 5 minutes.
4. Add sun-dried tomatoes and olives.
5. Beat eggs with herbs, salt, and pepper.
6. Pour eggs over vegetables and cook for 3 minutes.
7. Transfer to oven and bake 15-20 minutes until set.

Ginger-Spiced Carrot Cake Overnight Oats

Prep Time: 10 minutes Chill Time: Overnight Serves: 2

1 cup rolled oats
1 cup unsweetened almond milk
1/2 cup grated carrots
2 tbsp ground flaxseed
1 tbsp chia seeds
1 tsp ground ginger
1/2 tsp ground cinnamon

1/4 tsp ground nutmeg
2 tbsp maple syrup
1/4 cup chopped walnuts
2 tbsp unsweetened coconut flakes

1. Mix all ingredients except nuts and coconut in a bowl.
2. Divide between two jars or containers.
3. Refrigerate overnight.
4. Top with walnuts and coconut before serving.

Smoked Mackerel and Cucumber Wraps

Prep Time: 10 minutes Serves: 2

2 large collard green leaves or coconut wraps
4 oz smoked mackerel, flaked
1/2 cucumber, julienned
1/2 avocado, sliced
2 tbsp fresh dill
1 tbsp capers

2 tbsp extra virgin olive oil
1 tbsp lemon juice
Mixed greens
Black pepper to taste

1. Remove stems from collard leaves and blanch briefly if desired.
2. Mix mackerel with olive oil, lemon juice, dill, and capers.
3. Layer greens, mackerel mixture, cucumber, and avocado on wraps.
4. Roll tightly and slice in half.

Green Juice with Protein

Prep Time: 10 minutes Serves: 1

2 cups fresh spinach
1 cucumber
1 green apple
1 inch fresh ginger
1/2 lemon, juiced
1 tbsp hemp hearts
1 scoop plant-based protein powder
(optional)
1 cup coconut water
Ice cubes

1. Juice spinach, cucumber, apple, and ginger.
2. Add lemon juice and coconut water.
3. Blend with protein powder and hemp hearts if using.
4. Serve over ice.

Turmeric Coconut Rice Porridge

Prep Time: 5 minutes Cook Time: 20 minutes Serves: 2

1/2 cup short-grain brown rice
1 can (400ml) coconut milk
1 cup water
1 tsp ground turmeric
1/2 tsp ground ginger
1/4 tsp ground cardamom
2 tbsp raw honey
1/4 cup toasted coconut flakes
2 tbsp pistachios, chopped
Fresh mango slices

1. Combine rice, coconut milk, water, and spices in a saucepan.
2. Bring to a boil, then reduce heat and simmer 20 minutes.
3. Stir in honey.
4. Serve topped with coconut, pistachios, and mango.

Sardine and Tomato Toast

Prep Time: 8 minutes Serves: 2

2 slices sprouted grain bread
1 can (4 oz) sardines in olive oil
2 large tomatoes, sliced
1/4 red onion, thinly sliced
2 tbsp extra virgin olive oil
1 tbsp balsamic vinegar
2 tbsp fresh basil leaves
1 tbsp capers
Sea salt and black pepper

1. Toast bread until golden.
2. Drizzle with olive oil.
3. Layer tomatoes, sardines, onion, and capers.
4. Drizzle with balsamic vinegar.
5. Top with fresh basil and season.

Berry Chia Bowl

Prep Time: 10 minutes Serves: 1

3 tbsp chia seeds
1/2 cup unsweetened almond milk
1/2 cup mixed berries (fresh or
frozen)
1 tbsp goji berries
1 tbsp raw cacao nibs
1 tbsp almond butter
1 tsp raw honey
1 tbsp coconut flakes
Fresh mint leaves

1. Mix chia seeds with almond milk and let sit 10 minutes.
2. Layer chia mixture with berries in a bowl.
3. Top with goji berries, cacao nibs, almond butter, and coconut.
4. Drizzle with honey and garnish with mint.

Spiced Pumpkin Seed Granola Bowl

Prep Time: 5 minutes Cook Time: 20 minutes Serves: 4

1 cup pumpkin seeds
1/2 cup sunflower seeds
1/4 cup coconut flakes
2 tbsp coconut oil, melted
1 tbsp maple syrup
1 tsp ground cinnamon
1/2 tsp ground ginger
1/4 tsp ground cloves
Pinch of sea salt
Coconut yogurt for serving
Fresh berries

1. Preheat oven to 325°F (165°C).
2. Mix all dry ingredients.
3. Add coconut oil and maple syrup.
4. Spread on baking sheet and bake 15-20 minutes.
5. Serve over coconut yogurt with berries.

Herbed Zucchini and Mushroom Scramble

Prep Time: 10 minutes Cook Time: 12 minutes Serves: 2

4 eggs
1 medium zucchini, diced
1 cup mixed mushrooms, sliced
2 tbsp coconut oil
2 cloves garlic, minced
2 tbsp fresh thyme
2 tbsp fresh parsley
1 tbsp fresh chives
Sea salt and pepper
Avocado slices for serving

1. Heat coconut oil in a skillet over medium heat.
2. Sauté mushrooms until golden, about 5 minutes.
3. Add zucchini and garlic, cook 3 minutes.
4. Add herbs and scrambled eggs.
5. Cook until eggs are just set.
6. Serve with avocado slices.

Coconut Chia Pancakes

Prep Time: 10 minutes Cook Time: 15 minutes Serves: 2

1/4 cup coconut flour
2 tbsp chia seeds, ground
4 eggs
1/4 cup coconut milk
1 tbsp coconut oil, melted
1 tbsp raw honey
1/2 tsp vanilla extract
1/4 tsp baking soda
Pinch of sea salt
Coconut oil for cooking
Fresh berries for topping

1. Mix dry ingredients in a bowl.
2. Whisk wet ingredients separately.
3. Combine wet and dry ingredients.
4. Heat coconut oil in a pan over medium-low heat.
5. Cook pancakes 2-3 minutes per side.
6. Serve with fresh berries.

Omega-3 Rich Walnut Porridge

Prep Time: 5 minutes Cook Time: 10 minutes Serves: 2

1 cup raw walnuts, soaked
overnight
1 1/2 cups water
1/4 cup coconut milk
1 tbsp ground flaxseed
1 tbsp maple syrup
1/2 tsp vanilla extract
1/4 tsp ground cinnamon
Fresh berries and sliced almonds
for topping

1. Drain and rinse soaked walnuts.
2. Blend walnuts with water until smooth and creamy.
3. Pour into a saucepan and heat gently.
4. Add coconut milk, flaxseed, maple syrup, vanilla, and cinnamon.
5. Simmer 5 minutes, stirring frequently.
6. Serve topped with berries and almonds.

Breakfast Salad

Prep Time: 15 minutes Serves: 2

4 cups mixed greens (arugula,
spinach, kale)
2 soft-boiled eggs, halved
1/2 avocado, sliced
1/4 cup pomegranate seeds
2 tbsp hemp hearts
2 tbsp extra virgin olive oil
1 tbsp apple cider vinegar
1 tsp Dijon mustard
1 tbsp fresh lemon juice
Sea salt and pepper

1. Arrange greens in bowls.
2. Top with eggs, avocado, and pomegranate seeds.
3. Whisk together oil, vinegar, mustard, and lemon juice.
4. Drizzle dressing over salad.
5. Sprinkle with hemp hearts and season.

Golden Milk Overnight Oats

Prep Time: 10 minutes Chill Time: Overnight Serves: 2

1 cup rolled oats
1 cup coconut milk
1 tsp ground turmeric
1/2 tsp ground ginger
1/4 tsp ground cinnamon
Pinch of black pepper
2 tbsp chia seeds
2 tbsp maple syrup
1/4 cup chopped dates
Toasted coconut flakes and
pistachios for topping

1. Mix all ingredients except toppings in a bowl.
2. Divide between containers and refrigerate overnight.
3. Serve topped with coconut flakes and pistachios.

Probiotic Berry Parfait

Prep Time: 8 minutes Serves: 2

1 cup unsweetened coconut yogurt
1/2 cup mixed berries
2 tbsp ground flaxseed
2 tbsp chia seeds
1/4 cup walnuts, chopped
1 tbsp raw honey
1/2 tsp vanilla extract
1 tbsp coconut flakes
Fresh mint for garnish

1. Mix yogurt with honey and vanilla.
2. Layer yogurt, berries, flaxseed, and chia seeds in glasses.
3. Repeat layers.
4. Top with walnuts, coconut flakes, and mint.
5. Serve or chill for later.

LUNCH & LIGHT MEALS

Mediterranean Quinoa Power Bowl

Prep Time: 15 minutes Cook Time: 15 minutes Serves: 4

1 cup quinoa, rinsed
2 cups low-sodium vegetable broth
1 cucumber, diced
1 cup cherry tomatoes, halved
1/2 red onion, thinly sliced
1/2 cup kalamata olives, pitted
1/4 cup fresh parsley, chopped
1/4 cup fresh mint, chopped

4 oz feta cheese, crumbled
3 tbsp extra virgin olive oil
2 tbsp lemon juice
1 tsp dried oregano
2 cloves garlic, minced
Salt and pepper to taste

1. Cook quinoa in vegetable broth according to package directions. Let cool.
2. Whisk together olive oil, lemon juice, oregano, garlic, salt, and pepper.
3. Combine cooled quinoa with vegetables, herbs, and feta.
4. Toss with dressing and serve immediately or chill for later.

Turmeric-Ginger Carrot Soup

Prep Time: 10 minutes Cook Time: 25 minutes Serves: 4

2 lbs carrots, peeled and chopped
1 onion, diced
3 cloves garlic, minced
2 inches fresh ginger, grated
1 tsp ground turmeric
4 cups low-sodium vegetable broth

1 can (14oz) coconut milk
2 tbsp olive oil
1 tsp ground cumin
Salt and pepper to taste
Fresh cilantro for garnish

1. Heat olive oil in a large pot. Sauté onion until softened, about 5 minutes.
2. Add garlic, ginger, turmeric, and cumin. Cook for 1 minute.
3. Add carrots and broth. Bring to boil, reduce heat, and simmer 20 minutes.
4. Blend until smooth. Stir in coconut milk and season with salt and pepper.
5. Garnish with fresh cilantro.

Wild Salmon and Avocado Lettuce Wraps

Prep Time: 15 minutes Cook Time: 8 minutes Serves: 2

8 oz wild salmon fillet
1 head butter lettuce, leaves
separated
1 large avocado, sliced
1 cucumber, julienned
1 cup shredded purple cabbage
1/4 cup fresh dill, chopped
2 tbsp olive oil
1 tbsp lemon juice
1 tsp Dijon mustard
Salt and pepper to taste

1. Season salmon with salt and pepper. Cook in 1 tbsp olive oil for 3-4 minutes per side.
2. Let salmon cool, then flake into bite-sized pieces.
3. Whisk together remaining olive oil, lemon juice, and mustard.
4. Fill lettuce leaves with salmon, avocado, cucumber, and cabbage.
5. Drizzle with dressing and sprinkle with dill.

Lentil and Vegetable Curry Bowl

Prep Time: 15 minutes Cook Time: 30 minutes Serves: 4

1 cup red lentils, rinsed
2 cups low-sodium vegetable broth
1 can (14oz) coconut milk
1 onion, diced
2 cloves garlic, minced
1 tbsp fresh ginger, grated
1 tsp ground turmeric
1 tsp ground cumin
1 tsp ground coriander
2 cups spinach, chopped
1 red bell pepper, diced
2 tbsp coconut oil
Salt to taste
Fresh cilantro for garnish

1. Heat coconut oil in a large pot. Sauté onion until soft.
2. Add garlic, ginger, and spices. Cook for 1 minute.
3. Add lentils, broth, and coconut milk. Bring to boil.
4. Reduce heat and simmer 20 minutes until lentils are tender.
5. Stir in bell pepper and spinach. Cook 5 minutes more.
6. Season with salt and garnish with cilantro.

Grilled Vegetable and Hummus Wrap

Prep Time: 20 minutes Cook Time: 15 minutes Serves: 2

2 large whole wheat tortillas
1 zucchini, sliced lengthwise
1 red bell pepper, cut in strips
1 yellow bell pepper, cut in strips
1 small eggplant, sliced
1/2 cup homemade or high-quality
hummus
2 tbsp olive oil
1 tsp dried herbs (oregano, thyme)
2 cups arugula
1/4 cup sun-dried tomatoes,
chopped
Salt and pepper to taste

1. Brush vegetables with olive oil and season with herbs, salt, and pepper.
2. Grill vegetables 3-4 minutes per side until tender and lightly charred.
3. Warm tortillas slightly.
4. Spread hummus on tortillas, add grilled vegetables, arugula, and sun-dried tomatoes.
5. Roll tightly and cut in half.

Asian-Style Ginger Bok Choy Soup

Prep Time: 10 minutes Cook Time: 15 minutes Serves: 3

4 cups low-sodium vegetable broth
2 inches fresh ginger, sliced
3 cloves garlic, sliced
1 lb baby bok choy, chopped
1 cup shiitake mushrooms, sliced
1 block (14oz) firm tofu, cubed
2 green onions, sliced
2 tbsp coconut aminos or low-
sodium soy sauce
1 tbsp sesame oil
1 tsp rice vinegar
Red pepper flakes to taste

1. Bring broth to simmer with ginger and garlic slices.
2. Add mushrooms and cook 5 minutes.
3. Add bok choy and tofu, cook 3-4 minutes until bok choy is tender.
4. Remove ginger slices. Stir in coconut aminos, sesame oil, and vinegar.
5. Garnish with green onions and red pepper flakes.

Chickpea and Vegetable Stir-Fry

Prep Time: 15 minutes Cook Time: 12 minutes Serves: 3

1 can (15oz) chickpeas, drained and rinsed
2 tbsp coconut oil
1 red bell pepper, sliced
1 yellow bell pepper, sliced
1 cup broccoli florets
1 carrot, julienned
2 cloves garlic, minced
1 tbsp fresh ginger, grated
2 tbsp coconut aminos

1 tbsp lime juice
1 tsp ground turmeric
1/4 cup fresh cilantro, chopped
2 tbsp pumpkin seeds

1. Heat coconut oil in a large skillet or wok.
2. Add chickpeas and cook 3-4 minutes until lightly crispy.
3. Add vegetables, garlic, and ginger. Stir-fry 5-6 minutes.
4. Mix coconut aminos, lime juice, and turmeric. Pour over vegetables.
5. Cook 2 minutes more. Garnish with cilantro and pumpkin seeds.

Kale and Sweet Potato Salad

Prep Time: 15 minutes Cook Time: 25 minutes Serves: 4

2 large sweet potatoes, cubed
6 cups kale, stems removed,
chopped
1/2 cup walnuts, chopped
1/2 cup dried cranberries
(unsweetened)
1/4 cup pumpkin seeds
3 tbsp olive oil
2 tbsp apple cider vinegar
1 tbsp honey
1 tsp Dijon mustard
Salt and pepper to taste

1. Roast sweet potato cubes with 1 tbsp olive oil at 400°F for 25 minutes.
2. Massage chopped kale with a pinch of salt until softened.
3. Whisk together remaining olive oil, vinegar, honey, and mustard.
4. Combine kale with roasted sweet potatoes, walnuts, cranberries, and pumpkin seeds.
5. Toss with dressing before serving.

Herb-Crusted Baked Cod with Vegetables

Prep Time: 15 minutes Cook Time: 20 minutes Serves: 2

2 cod fillets (6oz each)
1 zucchini, sliced
1 yellow squash, sliced
1 cup cherry tomatoes
1/4 cup fresh parsley, chopped
2 tbsp fresh dill, chopped
3 tbsp olive oil
2 cloves garlic, minced
1 lemon, juiced and zested
Salt and pepper to taste

1. Preheat oven to 400°F.
2. Mix herbs, garlic, olive oil, lemon juice, and zest.
3. Place cod and vegetables on baking sheet. Drizzle with herb mixture.
4. Season with salt and pepper.
5. Bake 15-20 minutes until fish flakes easily.

Quinoa-Stuffed Bell Peppers

Prep Time: 20 minutes Cook Time: 35 minutes Serves: 4

4 large bell peppers, tops cut,
seeds removed
1 cup cooked quinoa
1/2 cup black beans, rinsed
1/2 cup corn kernels
1/4 cup red onion, diced
1/4 cup cilantro, chopped
2 tbsp olive oil
1 tbsp lime juice
1 tsp ground cumin
1/2 tsp paprika
Salt and pepper to taste
1/4 cup pumpkin seeds

1. Preheat oven to 375°F.
2. Mix quinoa, black beans, corn, onion, cilantro, olive oil, lime juice, and spices.
3. Stuff peppers with quinoa mixture.
4. Place in baking dish with 1/4 inch water. Cover with foil.
5. Bake 30 minutes. Remove foil, top with pumpkin seeds, bake 5 minutes more.

Miso-Glazed Salmon with Steamed Vegetables

Prep Time: 10 minutes Cook Time: 15 minutes Serves: 2

2 salmon fillets (6oz each)
2 tbsp white miso paste
1 tbsp rice vinegar
1 tbsp honey
1 tsp sesame oil
2 cups broccoli florets
1 cup snap peas
1 carrot, sliced diagonally
1 tbsp coconut oil
1 tsp fresh ginger, grated
Sesame seeds for garnish

1. Mix miso, vinegar, honey, and sesame oil for glaze.
2. Brush salmon with glaze. Let marinate 10 minutes.
3. Steam vegetables until tender-crisp, about 5-7 minutes.
4. Cook salmon in coconut oil 4-5 minutes per side.
5. Toss vegetables with ginger. Serve with salmon, garnish with sesame seeds.

Mediterranean Chickpea Salad

Prep Time: 15 minutes Cook Time: None Serves: 4

2 cans (15oz each) chickpeas,
drained and rinsed
1 cucumber, diced
1 cup cherry tomatoes, halved
1/2 red onion, thinly sliced
1/2 cup kalamata olives, pitted and
halved
1/4 cup fresh parsley, chopped
2 tbsp fresh oregano, chopped
1/4 cup olive oil
3 tbsp lemon juice
2 cloves garlic, minced
Salt and pepper to taste

1. Combine chickpeas, cucumber, tomatoes, onion, olives, and herbs in a
large bowl.
2. Whisk together olive oil, lemon juice, garlic, salt, and pepper.
3. Pour dressing over salad and toss well.
4. Let sit 15 minutes for flavors to meld before serving.

Thai-Style Coconut Vegetable Soup

Prep Time: 15 minutes Cook Time: 20 minutes Serves: 4

1 can (14oz) coconut milk
2 cups vegetable broth
2 stalks lemongrass, bruised
3 kaffir lime leaves (or lime zest)
2 inches galangal or ginger, sliced
2 Thai chilies, sliced (optional)
1 cup mushrooms, sliced
1 red bell pepper, sliced

1 cup baby spinach
2 tbsp lime juice
2 tbsp coconut aminos
Fresh cilantro and basil for garnish

1. Simmer coconut milk, broth, lemongrass, lime leaves, and galangal for 10 minutes.
2. Strain out aromatics or leave in for stronger flavor.
3. Add mushrooms and bell pepper. Cook 5 minutes.
4. Stir in spinach, lime juice, and coconut aminos.
5. Garnish with fresh herbs.

Roasted Vegetable and Hummus Bowl

Prep Time: 15 minutes Cook Time: 30 minutes Serves: 2

1 sweet potato, cubed
1 red bell pepper, sliced
1 zucchini, sliced
1 red onion, sliced
2 cups Brussels sprouts, halved
3 tbsp olive oil
1 tsp ground cumin
1 tsp paprika
1/2 cup hummus

2 tbsp tahini
1 tbsp lemon juice
2 cups arugula
1/4 cup pumpkin seeds

1. Preheat oven to 425°F.
2. Toss vegetables with olive oil, cumin, paprika, salt, and pepper.
3. Roast 25-30 minutes until tender and caramelized.
4. Mix tahini with lemon juice and a splash of water for drizzle.
5. Serve roasted vegetables over arugula with hummus and tahini drizzle.
Top with pumpkin seeds.

Sardine and Avocado Toast

Prep Time: 10 minutes Cook Time: None Serves: 2

4 slices whole grain sourdough
bread
2 cans (4oz each) wild sardines in
olive oil
2 ripe avocados
1 lemon, juiced
2 tbsp olive oil
1/4 red onion, thinly sliced
2 tbsp capers
2 tbsp fresh dill, chopped
Red pepper flakes to taste
Salt and pepper to taste

1. Toast bread until golden.
2. Mash avocados with lemon juice, salt, and pepper.
3. Spread avocado mixture on toast.
4. Top with sardines, red onion, capers, and dill.
5. Drizzle with olive oil and sprinkle with red pepper flakes.

Turmeric Cauliflower Rice Bowl

Prep Time: 15 minutes Cook Time: 15 minutes Serves: 3

1 large head cauliflower, riced
2 tbsp coconut oil
1 onion, diced
3 cloves garlic, minced
1 tbsp fresh ginger, grated
1 tsp ground turmeric
1/2 tsp ground cumin
1 cup cherry tomatoes, halved
1 cup baby spinach

1/4 cup cilantro, chopped
2 tbsp pumpkin seeds
Salt and pepper to taste

1. Rice cauliflower in food processor or grate by hand.
2. Heat coconut oil in large skillet. Sauté onion until soft.
3. Add garlic, ginger, turmeric, and cumin. Cook 1 minute.
4. Add cauliflower rice and cook 5-7 minutes.
5. Stir in tomatoes and spinach. Cook until spinach wilts.
6. Season with salt and pepper. Garnish with cilantro and pumpkin seeds.

Black Bean and Sweet Potato Quesadillas

Prep Time: 15 minutes Cook Time: 20 minutes Serves: 2

2 large sweet potatoes, diced small
1 can (15oz) black beans, drained
4 whole wheat tortillas
1/2 cup shredded cheese (optional)
1 bell pepper, diced
1/4 cup red onion, diced
2 tbsp olive oil
1 tsp ground cumin
1 tsp chili powder
1/4 cup cilantro, chopped
1 avocado, sliced

1. Roast sweet potatoes with 1 tbsp olive oil at 400°F for 15 minutes.
2. Mix roasted sweet potatoes with black beans, bell pepper, onion, cumin, and chili powder.
3. Fill tortillas with mixture and cheese if using.
4. Cook quesadillas in remaining olive oil, 2-3 minutes per side.
5. Serve with avocado and cilantro.

Greek-Style Lentil Soup

Prep Time: 15 minutes Cook Time: 35 minutes Serves: 4

1 cup dried green lentils, rinsed
4 cups vegetable broth
1 onion, diced
2 carrots, diced
2 celery stalks, diced
4 cloves garlic, minced
1 can (14oz) diced tomatoes
3 tbsp olive oil

2 tbsp red wine vinegar
1 tsp dried oregano
1/2 cup fresh parsley, chopped
Salt and pepper to taste

1. Heat olive oil in large pot. Sauté onion, carrots, and celery until soft.
2. Add garlic and oregano. Cook 1 minute.
3. Add lentils, broth, and tomatoes. Bring to boil.
4. Reduce heat and simmer 25-30 minutes until lentils are tender.
5. Stir in vinegar and parsley. Season with salt and pepper.

Zucchini Noodles with Pesto and Cherry Tomatoes

Prep Time: 20 minutes Cook Time: 5 minutes Serves: 3

4 large zucchini, spiralized
2 cups fresh basil leaves
1/4 cup pine nuts
3 cloves garlic
1/2 cup olive oil
1/4 cup nutritional yeast (or parmesan)
2 cups cherry tomatoes, halved
1 tbsp olive oil for cooking
Salt and pepper to taste
Red pepper flakes (optional)

1. Make pesto by blending basil, pine nuts, garlic, olive oil, and nutritional yeast until smooth.
2. Heat 1 tbsp olive oil in large skillet.
3. Add cherry tomatoes and cook 2-3 minutes until softened.
4. Add zucchini noodles and cook 1-2 minutes until just tender.
5. Toss with pesto and serve.

Moroccan-Spiced Vegetable Tagine

Prep Time: 20 minutes Cook Time: 30 minutes Serves: 4

2 tbsp olive oil
1 onion, diced
3 cloves garlic, minced
1 tsp ground ginger
1 tsp ground cinnamon
1 tsp ground cumin
1/2 tsp ground turmeric
2 carrots, sliced
1 sweet potato, cubed

1 can (14oz) diced tomatoes
1 can (15oz) chickpeas, drained
1/2 cup dried apricots, chopped
2 cups vegetable broth
1/4 cup almonds, sliced
Fresh cilantro for garnish

1. Heat olive oil in large pot. Sauté onion until soft.
2. Add garlic and spices. Cook 1 minute.
3. Add carrots, sweet potato, tomatoes, chickpeas, apricots, and broth.
4. Bring to boil, reduce heat, and simmer 25 minutes until vegetables are tender.
5. Garnish with almonds and cilantro.

DINNER & MAIN COURSE

The Meal Plan My Doctor Should Have Given me

Turmeric-Ginger Salmon with Roasted Rainbow Vegetables

Prep Time: 15 minutes Cook Time: 25 minutes Serves: 4

4 wild-caught salmon fillets (6 oz each)
2 tbsp fresh turmeric, grated (or 2 tsp ground)
1 tbsp fresh ginger, minced
3 tbsp extra virgin olive oil, divided
2 cups broccoli florets
1 red bell pepper, sliced
1 yellow bell pepper, sliced
1 zucchini, sliced

1 red onion, sliced
2 cloves garlic, minced
Sea salt and black pepper to taste
Lemon wedges for serving

1. Preheat oven to 425°F. Line a large baking sheet with parchment paper.
2. Mix turmeric, ginger, 1 tbsp olive oil, salt, and pepper. Rub over salmon fillets.
3. Toss vegetables with remaining olive oil, garlic, salt, and pepper.
4. Arrange vegetables on one side of the baking sheet, salmon on the other.
5. Bake for 15-18 minutes until salmon flakes easily and vegetables are tender.
6. Serve with lemon wedges.

Mediterranean Stuffed Sweet Potatoes

Prep Time: 10 minutes Cook Time: 50 minutes Serves: 4

4 large sweet potatoes
1 can (15 oz) chickpeas, drained
and rinsed
1 cup cherry tomatoes, halved
1/2 cup Kalamata olives, pitted and
sliced
1/4 cup red onion, diced
1/4 cup fresh parsley, chopped
2 tbsp fresh dill, chopped
3 tbsp extra virgin olive oil
2 tbsp lemon juice

2 cloves garlic, minced
1/4 cup tahini
Sea salt and pepper to taste

1. Preheat oven to 400°F. Pierce sweet potatoes and bake for 45-50 minutes until tender.
2. Meanwhile, combine chickpeas, tomatoes, olives, onion, parsley, and dill in a bowl.
3. Whisk together olive oil, lemon juice, garlic, salt, and pepper. Toss with chickpea mixture.
4. Cut open sweet potatoes, fluff flesh, and top with chickpea mixture.
5. Drizzle with tahini before serving.

Asian-Inspired Ginger-Garlic Chicken with Bok Choy

Prep Time: 15 minutes Cook Time: 20 minutes Serves: 4

1.5 lbs boneless, skinless chicken thighs, cut into strips
4 heads baby bok choy, halved lengthwise
2 tbsp coconut oil
3 tbsp fresh ginger, minced
4 cloves garlic, minced
2 green onions, sliced
2 tbsp coconut aminos
1 tbsp rice vinegar
1 tsp sesame oil

1/4 tsp red pepper flakes
2 tbsp sesame seeds
Fresh cilantro for garnish

1. Heat coconut oil in a large skillet over medium-high heat.
2. Add chicken and cook for 5-6 minutes until almost cooked through.
3. Add ginger and garlic, cook for 1 minute until fragrant.
4. Add bok choy, coconut aminos, vinegar, sesame oil, and red pepper flakes.
5. Cook for 3-4 minutes until bok choy is tender-crisp.
6. Garnish with green onions, sesame seeds, and cilantro.

Moroccan-Spiced Lentil and Vegetable Stew

Prep Time: 15 minutes Cook Time: 35 minutes Serves: 6

1.5 cups red lentils, rinsed
3 tbsp extra virgin olive oil
1 large onion, diced
3 carrots, diced
2 celery stalks, diced
4 cloves garlic, minced
2 tsp ground cumin
1 tsp ground coriander
1 tsp turmeric
1/2 tsp cinnamon

4 cups low-sodium vegetable broth
1 can (14.5 oz) diced tomatoes
2 cups fresh spinach
1/4 cup fresh cilantro, chopped
Sea salt and pepper to taste

1. Heat olive oil in a large pot over medium heat.
2. Add onion, carrots, and celery. Cook for 5 minutes until softened.
3. Add garlic and spices, cook for 1 minute until fragrant.
4. Add lentils, broth, and tomatoes. Bring to a boil.
5. Reduce heat, simmer covered for 20-25 minutes until lentils are tender.
6. Stir in spinach and cilantro, season with salt and pepper.

Herb-Crusted Cod with Roasted Asparagus

Prep Time: 10 minutes Cook Time: 20 minutes Serves: 4

4 cod fillets (6 oz each)
1 lb asparagus, trimmed
1/2 cup fresh parsley, chopped
1/4 cup fresh dill, chopped
2 tbsp fresh chives, chopped
3 tbsp extra virgin olive oil, divided
2 tbsp lemon juice
1 lemon, zested
2 cloves garlic, minced
Sea salt and pepper to taste

1. Preheat oven to 400°F. Line a baking sheet with parchment paper.
2. Toss asparagus with 1 tbsp olive oil, salt, and pepper. Arrange on baking sheet.
3. Mix herbs, remaining olive oil, lemon juice, zest, garlic, salt, and pepper.
4. Place cod on baking sheet with asparagus, top with herb mixture.
5. Bake for 15-18 minutes until fish flakes easily and asparagus is tender.

Coconut Curry Chicken with Cauliflower Rice

Prep Time: 15 minutes Cook Time: 25 minutes Serves: 4

1.5 lbs boneless chicken breasts, cubed
1 large head cauliflower, riced (or 4 cups pre-riced)
1 can (14 oz) full-fat coconut milk
2 tbsp coconut oil
1 large onion, diced
3 cloves garlic, minced
2 tbsp fresh ginger, minced
2 tbsp curry powder
1 tsp turmeric
1 bell pepper, diced

1 cup green beans, trimmed
Sea salt to taste
Fresh cilantro for garnish

1. Heat 1 tbsp coconut oil in a large skillet. Cook chicken until golden, set aside.
2. Add remaining oil, cook onion until softened.
3. Add garlic, ginger, curry powder, and turmeric. Cook 1 minute.
4. Add coconut milk, chicken, bell pepper, and green beans.
5. Simmer 15 minutes until vegetables are tender.
6. Steam cauliflower rice for 5 minutes. Serve curry over cauliflower rice.

Balsamic Glazed Portobello Mushroom Steaks

Prep Time: 10 minutes Cook Time: 15 minutes Serves: 4

4 large portobello mushroom caps,
stems removed
1/4 cup balsamic vinegar
2 tbsp extra virgin olive oil
2 cloves garlic, minced
1 tbsp fresh rosemary, chopped
4 cups mixed greens
1 avocado, sliced
1/4 cup walnuts, chopped
2 tbsp pumpkin seeds
Sea salt and pepper to taste

1. Preheat grill or grill pan to medium-high heat.
2. Mix balsamic vinegar, olive oil, garlic, rosemary, salt, and pepper.
3. Brush mushrooms with half the mixture, let marinate 5 minutes.
4. Grill mushrooms 4-5 minutes per side until tender.
5. Serve over mixed greens with avocado, walnuts, and pumpkin seeds.
6. Drizzle with remaining balsamic mixture.

Zucchini Noodles with Turkey Meatballs

Prep Time: 20 minutes Cook Time: 25 minutes Serves: 4

1 lb ground turkey (93% lean)
4 large zucchini, spiralized
1/4 cup almond flour
1 egg
2 cloves garlic, minced
1/4 cup fresh parsley, chopped
2 tbsp extra virgin olive oil
2 cups cherry tomatoes, halved
1/4 cup fresh basil, chopped
2 tbsp pine nuts
Sea salt and pepper to taste

1. Mix turkey, almond flour, egg, garlic, parsley, salt, and pepper. Form into 16 meatballs.
2. Heat olive oil in a large skillet. Brown meatballs on all sides, about 10 minutes.
3. Add cherry tomatoes, cook until they start to break down, about 5 minutes.
4. Add zucchini noodles, toss gently for 2-3 minutes until just tender.
5. Top with fresh basil and pine nuts before serving.

Thai-Inspired Coconut Fish Curry

Prep Time: 15 minutes Cook Time: 20 minutes Serves: 4

1.5 lbs white fish fillets (halibut or cod), cubed
1 can (14 oz) coconut milk
2 tbsp coconut oil
1 red bell pepper, sliced
1 yellow bell pepper, sliced
1 small eggplant, cubed
3 cloves garlic, minced
2 tbsp fresh ginger, minced
2 tbsp Thai curry paste (red or green)

1 tbsp fish sauce
1 lime, juiced
1/4 cup fresh cilantro
1/4 cup fresh basil

1. Heat coconut oil in a large pan over medium heat.
2. Add curry paste, cook for 1 minute until fragrant.
3. Add coconut milk, bring to a gentle simmer.
4. Add eggplant and bell peppers, cook for 8 minutes.
5. Add fish, garlic, and ginger. Cook 5-7 minutes until fish is cooked through.
6. Stir in fish sauce and lime juice. Garnish with herbs.

Mediterranean Quinoa-Stuffed Bell Peppers

Prep Time: 20 minutes Cook Time: 35 minutes Serves: 4

4 large bell peppers, tops cut off
and seeded
1 cup quinoa, cooked
1/2 cup sun-dried tomatoes,
chopped
1/4 cup Kalamata olives, chopped
1/4 cup pine nuts
1/4 cup fresh parsley, chopped
2 tbsp fresh dill, chopped
3 tbsp extra virgin olive oil
2 tbsp lemon juice
2 cloves garlic, minced
Sea salt and pepper to taste

1. Preheat oven to 375°F. Stand peppers in a baking dish.
2. Mix cooked quinoa, sun-dried tomatoes, olives, pine nuts, herbs, olive oil, lemon juice, garlic, salt, and pepper.
3. Stuff peppers with quinoa mixture.
4. Cover with foil and bake for 30-35 minutes until peppers are tender.
5. Remove foil for last 5 minutes to lightly brown tops.

Ginger-Soy Glazed Salmon with Steamed Broccoli

Prep Time: 10 minutes Cook Time: 15 minutes Serves: 4

4 salmon fillets (6 oz each)
4 cups broccoli florets
3 tbsp coconut aminos
2 tbsp rice vinegar
1 tbsp fresh ginger, grated
2 cloves garlic, minced
1 tbsp sesame oil
1 tbsp coconut oil
1 tsp honey
2 green onions, sliced
1 tbsp sesame seeds
Sea salt to taste

1. Steam broccoli for 5-7 minutes until tender-crisp, season with salt.
2. Mix coconut aminos, vinegar, ginger, garlic, sesame oil, and honey.
3. Heat coconut oil in a large skillet over medium-high heat.
4. Cook salmon skin-side up for 4 minutes, flip and cook 3 more minutes.
5. Pour glaze over salmon, cook 1 minute until thickened.
6. Serve salmon over broccoli, garnish with green onions and sesame seeds.

Roasted Vegetable and Lentil Bowl

Prep Time: 15 minutes Cook Time: 30 minutes Serves: 4

1 cup green lentils, cooked
2 sweet potatoes, cubed
2 beets, cubed
1 red onion, sliced
2 cups Brussels sprouts, halved
4 tbsp extra virgin olive oil, divided
2 tbsp balsamic vinegar
4 cups arugula
1/4 cup pumpkin seeds
1/4 cup dried cranberries
2 tbsp fresh thyme
Sea salt and pepper to taste

1. Preheat oven to 425°F. Line two baking sheets with parchment.
2. Toss sweet potatoes and beets with 2 tbsp olive oil, salt, and pepper. Roast 20 minutes.
3. Add Brussels sprouts and onion, roast 10 more minutes.
4. Whisk remaining olive oil with balsamic vinegar and thyme.
5. Serve roasted vegetables and lentils over arugula.
6. Top with pumpkin seeds and cranberries, drizzle with dressing.

Herb-Marinated Chicken with Ratatouille

Prep Time: 20 minutes + marinating Cook Time: 35 minutes Serves: 4

4 chicken breasts
1 eggplant, cubed
2 zucchini, cubed
1 red bell pepper, cubed
1 yellow bell pepper, cubed
1 large onion, diced
4 tomatoes, chopped
4 cloves garlic, minced
1/4 cup fresh basil, chopped
2 tbsp fresh oregano, chopped

4 tbsp extra virgin olive oil, divided
2 tbsp balsamic vinegar
Sea salt and pepper to taste

1. Marinate chicken in 2 tbsp olive oil, half the herbs, salt, and pepper for 30 minutes.
2. Heat 1 tbsp olive oil in a large skillet. Cook chicken 6-7 minutes per side, set aside.
3. Add remaining oil, cook onion until soft. Add eggplant, cook 5 minutes.
4. Add peppers and zucchini, cook 5 minutes. Add tomatoes and garlic, cook 10 minutes.
5. Stir in remaining herbs and balsamic vinegar.
6. Slice chicken and serve over ratatouille.

Coconut-Lime Shrimp with Cauliflower Rice

Prep Time: 15 minutes Cook Time: 10 minutes Serves: 4

1.5 lbs large shrimp, peeled and deveined
4 cups cauliflower rice
1 can (14 oz) coconut milk
2 tbsp coconut oil
1 red bell pepper, diced
1 jalapeño, minced
3 cloves garlic, minced
2 limes, juiced and zested
1/4 cup fresh cilantro, chopped

2 green onions, sliced
1 tsp ground cumin
Sea salt and pepper to taste

1. Heat 1 tbsp coconut oil in a large skillet. Sauté cauliflower rice for 5 minutes, season and set aside.
2. Heat remaining oil, add bell pepper and jalapeño, cook 3 minutes.
3. Add shrimp, garlic, and cumin. Cook 2-3 minutes until shrimp are pink.
4. Add coconut milk, lime juice, and zest. Simmer 2 minutes.
5. Serve shrimp over cauliflower rice, garnish with cilantro and green onions.

Baked Eggplant Parmesan (Dairy-Free)

Prep Time: 25 minutes Cook Time: 45 minutes Serves: 6

2 large eggplants, sliced into 1/2-inch rounds
2 cups almond flour
1/2 cup nutritional yeast
2 eggs, beaten
3 cups marinara sauce (no added sugar)
1/4 cup fresh basil, chopped
2 tbsp fresh oregano, chopped
3 tbsp extra virgin olive oil
2 cloves garlic, minced
Sea salt and pepper to taste

1. Preheat oven to 400°F. Salt eggplant slices, let sit 20 minutes, then pat dry.
2. Mix almond flour, nutritional yeast, salt, and pepper.
3. Dip eggplant in beaten eggs, then almond flour mixture.
4. Arrange on baking sheets, drizzle with olive oil. Bake 20 minutes, flipping once.
5. Layer eggplant with marinara sauce and herbs in a baking dish.
6. Bake 20-25 minutes until bubbly.

Turkey and Vegetable Chili

Prep Time: 15 minutes Cook Time: 45 minutes Serves: 6

1.5 lbs ground turkey (93% lean)
2 bell peppers, diced
1 large onion, diced
3 celery stalks, diced
3 carrots, diced
4 cloves garlic, minced
2 cans (14.5 oz each) diced tomatoes
1 can (15 oz) black beans, drained
2 cups low-sodium chicken broth
2 tbsp chili powder

1 tbsp cumin
1 tsp smoked paprika
2 tbsp extra virgin olive oil
Sea salt and pepper to taste
Avocado slices for serving

1. Heat olive oil in a large pot. Brown turkey, breaking it up as it cooks.
2. Add onion, bell peppers, celery, and carrots. Cook 8 minutes until softened.
3. Add garlic and spices, cook 1 minute until fragrant.
4. Add tomatoes, beans, and broth. Bring to a boil.
5. Reduce heat, simmer covered for 30 minutes.
6. Season with salt and pepper, serve topped with avocado.

Sesame-Crusted Tuna with Asian Slaw

Prep Time: 20 minutes Cook Time: 5 minutes Serves: 4

4 tuna steaks (6 oz each)
1/4 cup sesame seeds
4 cups shredded cabbage
2 carrots, julienned
1 red bell pepper, julienned
1/4 cup fresh cilantro, chopped
3 tbsp rice vinegar
2 tbsp sesame oil
1 tbsp coconut aminos

1 tbsp fresh ginger, grated
2 cloves garlic, minced
1 tbsp coconut oil
Sea salt and pepper to taste

1. Mix cabbage, carrots, bell pepper, and cilantro for slaw.
2. Whisk rice vinegar, sesame oil, coconut aminos, ginger, and garlic.
Toss with slaw.
3. Season tuna with salt and pepper, coat with sesame seeds.
4. Heat coconut oil in a skillet over high heat.
5. Sear tuna 1-2 minutes per side for rare, longer for more doneness.
6. Slice tuna and serve over Asian slaw.

Stuffed Acorn Squash with Wild Rice

Prep Time: 20 minutes Cook Time: 1 hour Serves: 4

2 large acorn squash, halved and
seeded
1 cup wild rice, cooked
1/2 cup dried cranberries
1/2 cup walnuts, chopped
1/4 cup fresh parsley, chopped
2 tbsp fresh sage, chopped
1 small onion, diced
2 celery stalks, diced
3 tbsp extra virgin olive oil, divided
2 tbsp balsamic vinegar
Sea salt and pepper to taste

1. Preheat oven to 400°F. Brush squash with 1 tbsp olive oil, season with
salt and pepper.
2. Roast cut-side down for 30 minutes, then flip and roast 15 more
minutes.
3. Heat remaining oil in a skillet. Sauté onion and celery until soft.
4. Mix cooked wild rice, sautéed vegetables, cranberries, walnuts, herbs,
and balsamic vinegar.
5. Fill squash halves with rice mixture.
6. Bake 10 more minutes until heated through.

Garlic-Herb Lamb Chops with Roasted Root Vegetables

Prep Time: 15 minutes Cook Time: 30 minutes Serves: 4

---

8 lamb chops (4 oz each)
3 large carrots, chunked
2 parsnips, chunked
2 beets, chunked
1 sweet potato, chunked
4 cloves garlic, minced
3 tbsp fresh rosemary, chopped
2 tbsp fresh thyme, chopped
4 tbsp extra virgin olive oil, divided
2 tbsp balsamic vinegar
Sea salt and pepper to taste

1. Preheat oven to 425°F. Toss root vegetables with 2 tbsp olive oil, salt, and pepper.
2. Roast vegetables for 25-30 minutes until tender.
3. Mix garlic, herbs, remaining olive oil, salt, and pepper. Rub over lamb chops.
4. Heat a grill pan over medium-high heat. Cook lamb chops 3-4 minutes per side for medium-rare.
5. Let lamb rest 5 minutes before serving.
6. Drizzle vegetables with balsamic vinegar before serving with lamb.

Mediterranean Vegetable and White Bean Stew

Prep Time: 15 minutes Cook Time: 35 minutes Serves: 6

2 cans (15 oz each) cannellini beans, drained
1 large eggplant, cubed
2 zucchini, cubed
1 red bell pepper, cubed
1 yellow bell pepper, cubed
1 large onion, diced
4 tomatoes, chopped
4 cloves garlic, minced
4 cups vegetable broth

1/4 cup fresh basil, chopped
2 tbsp fresh oregano, chopped
4 tbsp extra virgin olive oil
2 tbsp tomato paste
Sea salt and pepper to taste

1. Heat olive oil in a large pot over medium heat.
2. Add onion, cook until softened, about 5 minutes.
3. Add eggplant, cook 5 minutes. Add bell peppers and zucchini, cook 5 minutes.
4. Add garlic and tomato paste, cook 1 minute until fragrant.
5. Add tomatoes, beans, and broth. Bring to a boil.
6. Reduce heat, simmer 20 minutes. Stir in fresh herbs before serving.

SOUPS & STEWS

Golden Turmeric Chicken & Vegetable Soup

Prep Time: 15 minutes Cook Time: 35 minutes Serves: 6

2 lbs organic chicken thighs, bone-in, skin removed
8 cups low-sodium chicken bone broth
2 tbsp extra virgin olive oil
1 large onion, diced
3 carrots, sliced
3 celery stalks, chopped
4 garlic cloves, minced
2 tsp fresh turmeric (or 1 tsp dried)
1 tsp fresh ginger, grated

1 tsp ground cumin
1/2 tsp black pepper
2 cups baby spinach
1/4 cup fresh cilantro, chopped
1 lemon, juiced
Sea salt to taste

1. Heat olive oil in a large pot over medium heat. Add onions, carrots, and celery. Cook for 5 minutes until softened.
2. Add garlic, turmeric, ginger, cumin, and black pepper. Cook for 1 minute until fragrant.
3. Add chicken thighs and bone broth. Bring to a boil, then reduce heat and simmer for 25 minutes.
4. Remove chicken, shred meat, discard bones, and return meat to pot.
5. Stir in spinach until wilted. Add cilantro and lemon juice.
6. Season with sea salt and serve hot.

Mediterranean White Bean & Kale Stew

Prep Time: 10 minutes Cook Time: 25 minutes Serves: 4

3 tbsp extra virgin olive oil
1 large onion, diced
4 garlic cloves, minced
1 red bell pepper, chopped
2 cans (15 oz each) cannellini
beans, drained and rinsed
4 cups vegetable broth
1 can (14 oz) diced tomatoes
4 cups fresh kale, stems removed,
chopped
2 tsp dried oregano
1 tsp dried thyme

1/2 tsp smoked paprika
1/4 tsp red pepper flakes
2 bay leaves
Sea salt and black pepper to taste
Fresh parsley for garnish

1. Heat olive oil in a large pot over medium heat. Add onion and cook for 3 minutes.
2. Add garlic and red bell pepper, cook for 2 minutes.
3. Add beans, broth, diced tomatoes, oregano, thyme, paprika, red pepper flakes, and bay leaves.
4. Bring to a boil, then simmer for 15 minutes.
5. Stir in kale and cook until wilted, about 3 minutes.
6. Remove bay leaves, season with salt and pepper, and garnish with fresh parsley.

Healing Ginger-Miso Vegetable Soup

Prep Time: 15 minutes Cook Time: 20 minutes Serves: 4

6 cups vegetable broth
3 tbsp fresh ginger, minced
3 tbsp white miso paste
2 tbsp coconut aminos
1 tbsp sesame oil
8 oz shiitake mushrooms, sliced
1 red bell pepper, julienned
1 cup snap peas
4 baby bok choy, halved
3 green onions, sliced

1 sheet nori, cut into strips
1 tbsp sesame seeds
Fresh cilantro for garnish

1. In a large pot, bring vegetable broth and ginger to a boil. Reduce heat and simmer for 5 minutes.
2. In a small bowl, whisk miso paste with 1/2 cup of the hot broth until smooth. Return to pot.
3. Add coconut aminos and sesame oil.
4. Add mushrooms and bell pepper, cook for 5 minutes.
5. Add snap peas and bok choy, cook for 3 minutes until tender-crisp.
6. Serve topped with green onions, nori strips, sesame seeds, and cilantro.

Moroccan-Spiced Red Lentil Stew

Prep Time: 10 minutes Cook Time: 30 minutes Serves: 6

2 tbsp extra virgin olive oil
1 large onion, diced
4 garlic cloves, minced
2 tsp ground cumin
2 tsp ground coriander
1 tsp ground cinnamon
1 tsp turmeric
1/2 tsp cayenne pepper
1½ cups red lentils, rinsed
4 cups vegetable broth
1 can (14 oz) diced tomatoes

2 cups butternut squash, cubed
1 cup carrots, diced
1/2 cup dried apricots, chopped
2 tbsp tomato paste
Sea salt to taste
Fresh mint and cilantro for garnish

1. Heat olive oil in a large pot over medium heat. Add onion and cook for 5 minutes.
2. Add garlic and all spices, cook for 1 minute until fragrant.
3. Add lentils, broth, diced tomatoes, squash, carrots, apricots, and tomato paste.
4. Bring to a boil, then reduce heat and simmer for 20-25 minutes until lentils are tender.
5. Season with salt and serve garnished with fresh herbs.

Wild Salmon & Sweet Potato Chowder

Prep Time: 15 minutes Cook Time: 30 minutes Serves: 4

2 tbsp avocado oil
1 large leek, white and light green parts, sliced
2 celery stalks, diced
3 medium sweet potatoes, cubed
4 cups vegetable broth
1 can (14 oz) full-fat coconut milk
1 lb wild salmon fillet, skin removed, cut into chunks
1 cup frozen corn
2 tsp fresh thyme
1 tsp smoked paprika

1/2 tsp sea salt
1/4 tsp black pepper
2 tbsp fresh dill, chopped
Lemon wedges for serving

1. Heat avocado oil in a large pot over medium heat. Add leek and celery, cook for 5 minutes.
2. Add sweet potatoes and broth. Bring to a boil, then simmer for 15 minutes until potatoes are tender.
3. Stir in coconut milk, salmon chunks, corn, thyme, and paprika.
4. Simmer gently for 8-10 minutes until salmon is cooked through.
5. Season with salt and pepper, garnish with fresh dill, and serve with lemon wedges.

Bone Broth Vegetable Soup with Fresh Herbs

Prep Time: 15 minutes Cook Time: 25 minutes Serves: 6

8 cups beef or chicken bone broth
2 tbsp extra virgin olive oil
1 large onion, diced
3 carrots, sliced
3 celery stalks, chopped
1 zucchini, diced
1 yellow squash, diced
4 garlic cloves, minced
2 cups green beans, trimmed and
cut into 1-inch pieces
2 cups cabbage, chopped

2 tsp dried Italian herbs
1/4 cup fresh parsley, chopped
2 tbsp fresh basil, chopped
Sea salt and pepper to taste

1. Heat olive oil in a large pot over medium heat. Add onion, carrots, and celery. Cook for 5 minutes.
2. Add zucchini, yellow squash, and garlic. Cook for 3 minutes.
3. Add bone broth, green beans, cabbage, and Italian herbs.
4. Bring to a boil, then simmer for 15 minutes until vegetables are tender.
5. Stir in fresh herbs and season with salt and pepper.

Thai-Inspired Coconut Curry Soup

Prep Time: 20 minutes Cook Time: 25 minutes Serves: 4

2 tbsp coconut oil
1 large onion, sliced
3 tbsp fresh ginger, minced
4 garlic cloves, minced
2 tbsp red curry paste (check for no sugar added)
2 cans (14 oz each) full-fat coconut milk
2 cups vegetable broth
1 lb chicken breast, cut into strips
1 red bell pepper, sliced
1 cup snap peas
8 oz mushrooms, sliced

2 tbsp coconut aminos
1 tbsp lime juice
1/4 cup fresh basil, torn
1/4 cup fresh cilantro, chopped
Lime wedges for serving

1. Heat coconut oil in a large pot over medium heat. Add onion and cook for 3 minutes.
2. Add ginger, garlic, and curry paste. Cook for 1 minute until fragrant.
3. Add coconut milk and broth, bring to a simmer.
4. Add chicken and cook for 10 minutes.
5. Add bell pepper, snap peas, and mushrooms. Cook for 5 minutes.
6. Stir in coconut aminos and lime juice.
7. Serve garnished with fresh herbs and lime wedges.

Mushroom & Barley Stew

Prep Time: 15 minutes Cook Time: 45 minutes Serves: 6

3 tbsp extra virgin olive oil
1 large onion, diced
4 garlic cloves, minced
1 lb mixed mushrooms (shiitake, cremini, oyster), sliced
1 cup pearl barley
6 cups vegetable broth
2 carrots, diced
2 celery stalks, diced
2 tsp fresh thyme

1 tsp dried rosemary
2 bay leaves
2 cups kale, chopped
1/4 cup fresh parsley, chopped
Sea salt and pepper to taste

1. Heat olive oil in a large pot over medium-high heat. Add onion and cook for 3 minutes.
2. Add garlic and mushrooms, cook for 8 minutes until mushrooms release their liquid.
3. Add barley, broth, carrots, celery, thyme, rosemary, and bay leaves.
4. Bring to a boil, then reduce heat and simmer for 30 minutes until barley is tender.
5. Stir in kale and cook until wilted, about 3 minutes.
6. Remove bay leaves, add parsley, and season with salt and pepper.

Brazilian Fish Stew (Moqueca-Style)

Prep Time: 15 minutes Cook Time: 20 minutes Serves: 4

2 tbsp avocado oil
1 large onion, sliced
1 red bell pepper, sliced
1 yellow bell pepper, sliced
4 garlic cloves, minced
2 tbsp fresh ginger, minced
1 can (14 oz) diced tomatoes
1 can (14 oz) full-fat coconut milk
1/2 cup vegetable broth
1½ lbs white fish (cod or halibut),
cut into chunks

1 tbsp lime juice
1 tsp smoked paprika
1/2 tsp cayenne pepper
Sea salt to taste
1/4 cup fresh cilantro, chopped
Lime wedges for serving

1. Heat avocado oil in a large pot over medium heat. Add onion and bell peppers, cook for 5 minutes.
2. Add garlic and ginger, cook for 1 minute.
3. Add tomatoes, coconut milk, broth, paprika, and cayenne. Simmer for 8 minutes.
4. Gently add fish chunks and cook for 6-8 minutes until fish flakes easily.
5. Stir in lime juice and season with salt.
6. Serve garnished with cilantro and lime wedges.

Healing Cabbage & Turkey Soup

Prep Time: 10 minutes Cook Time: 30 minutes Serves: 6

2 tbsp extra virgin olive oil
1 lb ground turkey (93% lean)
1 large onion, diced
4 garlic cloves, minced
6 cups chicken bone broth
4 cups green cabbage, chopped
2 carrots, diced
2 celery stalks, diced
1 can (14 oz) diced tomatoes

2 tsp dried oregano
1 tsp dried thyme
1 bay leaf
1/2 tsp sea salt
1/4 tsp black pepper
2 tbsp fresh parsley, chopped

1. Heat olive oil in a large pot over medium-high heat. Add ground turkey and cook for 8 minutes, breaking it up as it cooks.
2. Add onion and garlic, cook for 3 minutes.
3. Add broth, cabbage, carrots, celery, tomatoes, oregano, thyme, and bay leaf.
4. Bring to a boil, then reduce heat and simmer for 20 minutes until vegetables are tender.
5. Remove bay leaf, season with salt and pepper, and garnish with fresh parsley.

D R I N K S

& BEVERAGES

Golden Turmeric Latte

2 cups unsweetened coconut milk
(or almond milk)
1 tsp ground turmeric
1/2 tsp ground ginger
1/4 tsp cinnamon
Pinch of black pepper
1 tbsp raw honey or maple syrup
1/2 tsp vanilla extract
Optional: 1/4 tsp cardamom

1. Heat coconut milk in a small saucepan over medium heat until steaming (don't boil).
2. Whisk in turmeric, ginger, cinnamon, and black pepper until well combined.
3. Simmer for 3-4 minutes, whisking occasionally.
4. Remove from heat and stir in honey and vanilla.
5. Strain if desired for smoother texture, or enjoy rustic-style.
6. Serve warm

Green Goddess Smoothie

Prep Time: 5 minutes Serves: 1

2 cups fresh spinach
1/2 ripe avocado
1 cup unsweetened coconut water
1/2 frozen banana
1-inch piece fresh ginger, peeled
1 tbsp fresh lime juice
1 tsp chia seeds
Handful of ice
Optional: 1 tsp spirulina powder for
extra nutrients

1. Add coconut water and spinach to blender first.
2. Add remaining ingredients.
3. Blend on high for 60-90 seconds until completely smooth.
4. Taste and adjust sweetness with more banana if needed.
5. Pour into a glass and drink

Tart Cherry Recovery Drink

Prep Time: 3 minutes Serves: 1

1 cup pure tart cherry juice (no
sugar added)
1/2 cup sparkling water
1 tbsp fresh lemon juice
1 tsp raw honey (optional)
1/4 tsp vanilla extract
Ice cubes
Fresh mint leaves for garnish

1. Fill a glass with ice cubes.
2. Pour tart cherry juice over ice.
3. Add lemon juice, honey (if using), and vanilla.
4. Top with sparkling water and stir gently.
5. Garnish with fresh mint and serve immediately.
6. Best consumed within 30 minutes of intense exercise or 1 hour before
bed.

Ginger Lemon Immunity Shot

Prep Time: 10 minutes Serves: 4 shots

4-inch piece fresh ginger root,
peeled
2 large lemons, juiced
1 tbsp raw honey
Pinch of cayenne pepper
1/4 cup water

1. Grate ginger finely or process in a food processor.
2. Place grated ginger in a fine-mesh strainer over a bowl.
3. Press and squeeze to extract as much juice as possible.
4. Mix ginger juice with lemon juice, honey, and cayenne.
5. Add water to dilute slightly if too intense.
6. Pour into shot glasses and consume.
7. Store leftovers in fridge for up to 3 days.

Hibiscus Rose Tea

2 tbsp dried hibiscus flowers
1 tsp dried rose petals (food-grade)
2 cups water
1 tbsp raw honey
1 tbsp fresh lime juice
Optional: 1 cinnamon stick

1. Bring water to a boil in a small pot.
2. Add hibiscus flowers and rose petals (and cinnamon if using).
3. Remove from heat and steep for 8-10 minutes.
4. Strain into cups, pressing flowers to extract maximum flavor.
5. Stir in honey and lime juice.
6. Serve hot or let cool and serve over ice.
7. Can be made in larger batches and stored in fridge for up to 5 days.

Matcha Coconut Latte

Prep Time: 5 minutes Cook Time: 3 minutes Serves: 1

1 tsp high-quality matcha powder
1 cup full-fat coconut milk
1 tbsp coconut oil
1 tsp raw honey or maple syrup
1/4 tsp vanilla extract
Pinch of sea salt

1. Sift matcha powder into a small bowl to remove lumps.
2. Add 2 tbsp warm (not hot) coconut milk to matcha and whisk until smooth paste forms.
3. Heat remaining coconut milk in a small saucepan until steaming.
4. Whisk in coconut oil until melted and incorporated.
5. Pour hot milk over matcha paste and whisk vigorously.
6. Add honey, vanilla, and salt. Stir well.
7. Pour into a mug.

Cucumber Mint Cooling Elixir

Prep Time: 10 minutes Serves: 2

2 large cucumbers, peeled and
chopped
1/4 cup fresh mint leaves
2 tbsp fresh lime juice
2 cups coconut water
1 tbsp raw honey (optional)
1/2 tsp fresh ginger, grated
Ice cubes
Cucumber slices and mint for
garnish

1. Blend chopped cucumbers until smooth.
2. Strain cucumber juice through fine-mesh strainer, pressing pulp to extract liquid.
3. In a pitcher, combine cucumber juice, coconut water, lime juice, and grated ginger.
4. Muddle mint leaves gently and add to pitcher.
5. Sweeten with honey if desired.
6. Serve over ice with cucumber slices and mint garnish.
7. Best consumed fresh, but can be stored in fridge for up to 2 days.

Bone Broth Turmeric Sipper

Prep Time: 5 minutes Cook Time: 10 minutes Serves: 2

2 cups high-quality bone broth
(chicken or beef)
1 tsp ground turmeric
1/2 tsp ground ginger
1/4 tsp garlic powder
1 tbsp coconut oil or ghee
1 tbsp fresh lemon juice
Sea salt and black pepper to taste
Fresh herbs (parsley or cilantro) for
garnish

1. Heat bone broth in a saucepan over medium heat.
2. Whisk in turmeric, ginger, and garlic powder.
3. Simmer for 5-8 minutes, whisking occasionally.
4. Remove from heat and whisk in coconut oil until melted.
5. Add lemon juice and season with salt and pepper.
6. Strain if desired for smoother consistency.
7. Serve hot, garnished with fresh herbs.

Pomegranate Ginger Sparkler

Prep Time: 5 minutes Serves: 2

1 cup 100% pomegranate juice
1 cup sparkling water
2 tbsp fresh lime juice
1 tbsp fresh ginger juice (or 1 tsp
grated ginger)
1 tbsp raw honey
Ice cubes
Pomegranate seeds and lime
wheels for garnish

1. In a small bowl, whisk together pomegranate juice, lime juice, ginger juice, and honey.
2. Fill glasses with ice cubes.
3. Divide pomegranate mixture between glasses.
4. Top with sparkling water and stir gently.
5. Garnish with pomegranate seeds and lime wheels.
6. Serve while bubbly.

Blueberry Basil Water

Prep Time: 5 minutes Serves: 4

4 cups filtered water
1 cup fresh blueberries
8-10 fresh basil leaves
1 lemon, sliced
1 tbsp raw honey (optional)
Ice cubes

1. Gently muddle blueberries in the bottom of a large pitcher to release some juices.
2. Add basil leaves and muddle lightly (don't over-muddle or it will become bitter).
3. Add lemon slices and fill pitcher with water.
4. Stir in honey if using sweeter version.
5. Refrigerate for at least 2 hours, preferably overnight.
6. Serve over ice, making sure to get some fruit and herbs in each glass.
7. Refill pitcher with water up to 2 more times before ingredients lose potency.

30-DAY ANTI-INFLAMMATORY MEAL PLAN

Week 1 (Days 1-7)

Day 1
- Breakfast: Golden Turmeric Chia Pudding (p. 83)
- Lunch: Mediterranean Quinoa Power Bowl (p. 103)
- Dinner: Turmeric-Ginger Salmon with Roasted Rainbow Vegetables (p. 124)
- Drink: Golden Turmeric Latte (p. 156)

Day 2
- Breakfast: Wild Salmon and Avocado Scramble (p. 84)
- Lunch: Turmeric-Ginger Carrot Soup (p. 104)
- Dinner: Mediterranean Stuffed Sweet Potatoes (p. 125)
- Drink: Green Goddess Smoothie (p. 157)

Day 3
- Breakfast: Green Smoothie Bowl (p. 85)
- Lunch: Wild Salmon and Avocado Lettuce Wraps (p. 105)
- Dinner: Asian-Inspired Ginger-Garlic Chicken with Bok Choy (p. 126)
- Drink: Ginger Lemon Immunity Shot (p. 159)

Day 4
- Breakfast: Sweet Potato and Kale Hash with Poached Eggs (p. 86)
- Lunch: Lentil and Vegetable Curry Bowl (p. 106)
- Dinner: Moroccan-Spiced Lentil and Vegetable Stew (p. 127)
- Drink: Hibiscus Rose Tea (p. 160)

Day 5
- Breakfast: Coconut Berry Quinoa Breakfast Bowl (p. 87)
- Lunch: Grilled Vegetable and Hummus Wrap (p. 107)
- Dinner: Herb-Crusted Cod with Roasted Asparagus (p. 128)
- Drink: Matcha Coconut Latte (p. 161)

Day 6
- Breakfast: Mediterranean Vegetable Frittata (p. 88)
- Lunch: Asian-Style Ginger Bok Choy Soup (p. 108)
- Dinner: Coconut Curry Chicken with Cauliflower Rice (p. 129)
- Drink: Cucumber Mint Cooling Elixir (p. 162)

Day 7
- Breakfast: Ginger-Spiced Carrot Cake Overnight Oats (p. 89)
- Lunch: Chickpea and Vegetable Stir-Fry (p. 109)
- Dinner: Balsamic Glazed Portobello Mushroom Steaks (p. 130)
- Drink: Tart Cherry Recovery Drink (p. 158)

Week 2 (Days 8-14)

Day 8
- Breakfast: Smoked Mackerel and Cucumber Wraps (p. 90)
- Lunch: Kale and Sweet Potato Salad (p. 110)
- Dinner: Zucchini Noodles with Turkey Meatballs (p. 131)
- Drink: Bone Broth Turmeric Sipper (p. 163)

Day 9
- Breakfast: Green Juice with Protein (p. 91)
- Lunch: Herb-Crusted Baked Cod with Vegetables (p. 111)
- Dinner: Thai-Inspired Coconut Fish Curry (p. 132)
- Drink: Pomegranate Ginger Sparkler (p. 164)

Day 10
- Breakfast: Turmeric Coconut Rice Porridge (p. 92)
- Lunch: Quinoa-Stuffed Bell Peppers (p. 112)
- Dinner: Mediterranean Quinoa-Stuffed Bell Peppers (p. 133)
- Drink: Blueberry Basil Water (p. 165)

Day 11
- Breakfast: Sardine and Tomato Toast (p. 93)
- Lunch: Miso-Glazed Salmon with Steamed Vegetables (p. 113)
- Dinner: Ginger-Soy Glazed Salmon with Steamed Broccoli (p. 134)
- Drink: Golden Turmeric Latte (p. 156)

Day 12
- Breakfast: Berry Chia Bowl (p. 94)
- Lunch: Mediterranean Chickpea Salad (p. 114)
- Dinner: Roasted Vegetable and Lentil Bowl (p. 135)
- Drink: Green Goddess Smoothie (p. 157)

Day 13
- Breakfast: Spiced Pumpkin Seed Granola Bowl (p. 95)
- Lunch: Thai-Style Coconut Vegetable Soup (p. 115)
- Dinner: Herb-Marinated Chicken with Ratatouille (p. 136)
- Drink: Matcha Coconut Latte (p. 161)

Day 14
- Breakfast: Herbed Zucchini and Mushroom Scramble (p. 96)
- Lunch: Roasted Vegetable and Hummus Bowl (p. 116)

- Dinner: Coconut-Lime Shrimp with Cauliflower Rice (p. 137)
- Drink: Hibiscus Rose Tea (p. 160)

Week 3 (Days 15-21)

Day 15
- Breakfast: Coconut Chia Pancakes (p. 97)
- Lunch: Sardine and Avocado Toast (p. 117)
- Dinner: Baked Eggplant Parmesan (Dairy-Free) (p. 138)
- Drink: Ginger Lemon Immunity Shot (p. 159)

Day 16
- Breakfast: Omega-3 Rich Walnut Porridge (p. 98)
- Lunch: Turmeric Cauliflower Rice Bowl (p. 118)
- Dinner: Turkey and Vegetable Chili (p. 139)
- Drink: Cucumber Mint Cooling Elixir (p. 162)

Day 17
- Breakfast: Breakfast Salad (p. 99)
- Lunch: Black Bean and Sweet Potato Quesadillas (p. 119)
- Dinner: Sesame-Crusted Tuna with Asian Slaw (p. 140)
- Drink: Tart Cherry Recovery Drink (p. 158)

Day 18
- Breakfast: Golden Milk Overnight Oats (p. 100)
- Lunch: Greek-Style Lentil Soup (p. 120)
- Dinner: Stuffed Acorn Squash with Wild Rice (p. 141)
- Drink: Bone Broth Turmeric Sipper (p. 163)

Day 19
- Breakfast: Probiotic Berry Parfait (p. 101)
- Lunch: Zucchini Noodles with Pesto and Cherry Tomatoes (p. 121)
- Dinner: Garlic-Herb Lamb Chops with Roasted Root Vegetables (p. 142)
- Drink: Pomegranate Ginger Sparkler (p. 164)

Day 20
- Breakfast: Golden Turmeric Chia Pudding (p. 83)
- Lunch: Moroccan-Spiced Vegetable Tagine (p. 122)
- Dinner: Mediterranean Vegetable and White Bean Stew (p. 143)
- Drink: Blueberry Basil Water (p. 165)

Day 21
- Breakfast: Wild Salmon and Avocado Scramble (p. 84)
- Lunch: Golden Turmeric Chicken & Vegetable Soup (p. 145)
- Dinner: Turmeric-Ginger Salmon with Roasted Rainbow Vegetables (p. 124)
- Drink: Golden Turmeric Latte (p. 156)

Week 4 (Days 22-28)

Day 22
- Breakfast: Green Smoothie Bowl (p. 85)
- Lunch: Mediterranean White Bean & Kale Stew (p. 146)
- Dinner: Asian-Inspired Ginger-Garlic Chicken with Bok Choy (p. 126)
- Drink: Green Goddess Smoothie (p. 157)

Day 23
- Breakfast: Sweet Potato and Kale Hash with Poached Eggs (p. 86)
- Lunch: Healing Ginger-Miso Vegetable Soup (p. 147)
- Dinner: Herb-Crusted Cod with Roasted Asparagus (p. 128)
- Drink: Matcha Coconut Latte (p. 161)

Day 24
- Breakfast: Coconut Berry Quinoa Breakfast Bowl (p. 87)
- Lunch: Moroccan-Spiced Red Lentil Stew (p. 148)
- Dinner: Coconut Curry Chicken with Cauliflower Rice (p. 129)
- Drink: Hibiscus Rose Tea (p. 160)

Day 25
- Breakfast: Mediterranean Vegetable Frittata (p. 88)
- Lunch: Wild Salmon & Sweet Potato Chowder (p. 149)
- Dinner: Mediterranean Stuffed Sweet Potatoes (p. 125)
- Drink: Ginger Lemon Immunity Shot (p. 159)

Day 26
- Breakfast: Ginger-Spiced Carrot Cake Overnight Oats (p. 89)
- Lunch: Bone Broth Vegetable Soup with Fresh Herbs (p. 150)
- Dinner: Thai-Inspired Coconut Fish Curry (p. 132)
- Drink: Cucumber Mint Cooling Elixir (p. 162)

Day 27
- Breakfast: Smoked Mackerel and Cucumber Wraps (p. 90)
- Lunch: Thai-Inspired Coconut Curry Soup (p. 151)
- Dinner: Zucchini Noodles with Turkey Meatballs (p. 131)
- Drink: Tart Cherry Recovery Drink (p. 158)

Day 28
- Breakfast: Green Juice with Protein (p. 91)
- Lunch: Mushroom & Barley Stew (p. 152)
- Dinner: Balsamic Glazed Portobello Mushroom Steaks (p. 130)
- Drink: Bone Broth Turmeric Sipper (p. 163)

Days 29-30 (Bonus Days)

Day 29
- Breakfast: Turmeric Coconut Rice Porridge (p. 92)
- Lunch: Brazilian Fish Stew (Moqueca-Style) (p. 153)
- Dinner: Coconut-Lime Shrimp with Cauliflower Rice (p. 137)
- Drink: Pomegranate Ginger Sparkler (p. 164)

Day 30
- Breakfast: Sardine and Tomato Toast (p. 93)
- Lunch: Healing Cabbage & Turkey Soup (p. 154)
- Dinner: Garlic-Herb Lamb Chops with Roasted Root Vegetables (p. 142)
- Drink: Golden Turmeric Latte (p. 156)

Key Anti-Inflammatory Benefits

This meal plan emphasizes:
- Omega-3 rich foods: Wild salmon, sardines, mackerel, walnuts
- Turmeric and ginger: Natural anti-inflammatory compounds
- Colorful vegetables: Rich in antioxidants and phytonutrients
- Leafy greens: High in vitamins and minerals
- Healthy fats: Avocado, coconut, olive oil
- Fiber-rich foods: Quinoa, lentils, beans, vegetables
- Herbs and spices: Natural anti-inflammatory compounds

Shopping Tips

- Batch prep ingredients on weekends
- Freeze portions of soups and stews
- Keep anti-inflammatory spices (turmeric, ginger, garlic) well-stocked
- Choose wild-caught fish when possible
- Opt for organic produce for the "Dirty Dozen" items
- Prepare overnight oats and chia puddings in advance

Hydration Reminders

In addition to the daily drink recipes, remember to:
- Drink plenty of water throughout the day
- Add lemon or cucumber to water for extra flavor
- Herbal teas count toward daily fluid intake
- Limit inflammatory beverages like alcohol and sugary drinks

The Meal Plan My Doctor Should Have Given me

Made in the USA
Middletown, DE
22 June 2025